PURBECK
PERSONALITIES

PURBECK
PERSONALITIES

DR ANDREW NORMAN

HALSGROVE

First published in Great Britain in 2009

Copyright © Andrew Norman 2009

British Library Cataloguing-in-Publication Data
A CIP record for this title is available from the British Library

ISBN 978 1 84114 900 4

HALSGROVE
Halsgrove House,
Ryelands Industrial Estate,
Bagley Road, Wellington, Somerset TA21 9PZ
Tel: 01823 653777   Fax: 01823 216796
email: sales@halsgrove.com

Part of the Halsgrove group of companies.
Information on all Halsgrove titles is available at: www.halsgrove.com

Printed and bound by The Cromwell Press Group, Trowbridge

Contents

Acknowledgements

English China Clays plc; National Portrait Gallery; The Oakwood Press; The Purbeck Mineral and Mining Museum; The Royal National Lifeboat Institution; The Wedgwood Museum, Barlaston, Stoke-on-Trent, Staffordshire/Keele University Special Collections and Archives; Swanage Museum and Heritage Centre; Madras College, St Andrews, Scotland.

Liz Agnew; Jennifer Barnard; Janet Brown; John Dean; David Haysom; Anthony Houghton; David Lewer; CD Pike; John Rowley; RJ Saville; Mary Spencer Watson; William Stockley.

I am deeply grateful to David Haysom of Swanage for all his help and expert advice. I am also deeply grateful, as always, to my beloved wife Rachel, for all her help and encouragement.

Preface

The Isle of Purbeck is an area of about 60 square miles, situated in South Dorset in southern England. Although bounded by sea to the south and east, and by Poole Harbour and the River Frome to the north, it is not strictly speaking an island at all. Nevertheless, to both local people and to the tourists, who come in droves each year to visit, it may safely be said that Purbeck resembles an island paradise.

For those who wish simply to enjoy the scenery, Purbeck can offer spectacular cliffs, a large variety of sea birds, sandy beaches, rolling hills, heathlands and forests, ancient churches, and the mighty (if ruined monument of) Corfe Castle as its 'jewel in the crown'. For those who wish to delve deeper, however, there are other treats in store.

Every region has its association with eminent, flamboyant, or notorious characters, and Purbeck is no exception. Here, pirates operated in the 16th century, and there was a smuggler in later years – who was also a churchwarden. In the 17th century, during the English Civil War, the wife of one of King Charles I's principal justices mounted a heroic defence of Corfe Castle during a prolonged siege. A Dorset farmer, who, though not a medical man, was the first person to inoculate against the deadly disease smallpox, came to Purbeck to live, and found an ally in the local rector, who was also one of the country's leading educationalists. Merchants mined the clay which Staffordshire potter Josiah Wedgwood, prized above all others. A quarry boy turned stone merchant from Swanage extracted, worked, and shipped the sought after Purbeck limestone (with which the streets of

London were paved,) and his nephew, also a stone merchant, brought back unwanted artefacts from London which cause interest and amusement in Swanage, even to this day. Purbeck had its share of tragedy, when, in 1895, the coxswain of the Swanage lifeboat was drowned on active service whilst attempting a daring rescue mission. In the 20th century, a distinguished painter and Fellow of the Royal Academy, painted his family set against the glorious backdrop of Purbeck.

Each of the above people contributed, in his or her unique way, towards creating the threads, of which the colourful tapestry of Purbeck is woven.

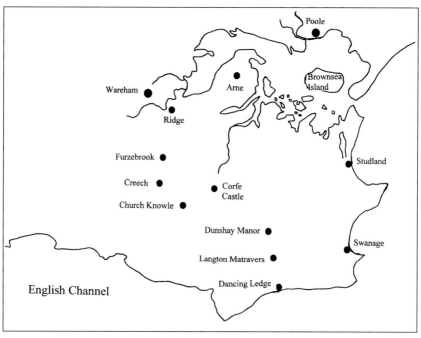

Dorset's Isle of Purbeck.

1

William Munday, Innkeeper of Studland and Friend of the Pirates

The village of Studland lies between South Haven Point and the entrance to Poole Harbour to the north, with Handfast Point and its pinnacle rocks – known as 'Old Harry' – to the south.

Studland's first church was built by the Anglo-Saxon scholar, prelate, and evangelist Aldhelm, first Bishop of Sherborne (who was later canonised) in the 7th century. The main body of this original church, including the walls of the nave and the base of the tower, were incorporated into the subsequent Church of St Nicholas, which was built by the Normans.

Studland is mentioned in the Domesday Book (the record of the great survey of England, which was completed in the year 1086 for the Norman King William I – where it is called 'Stollant',) as a place where salt-making was carried out.

Studland's beach is amongst the finest in England for its picturesqueness, and for the quality of its sand. From it, on a fine day, can be seen Bournemouth – 5 miles across the water to the north-east – and the Isle of Wight, 15 miles to the east. Here can be found sand dunes topped with marram grass, and the Studland Heath National Nature Reserve with its marshes and waterfowl, and an inland fresh-water lake, known as 'Little Sea'.

Today, for the reasons stated above, Studland is a magnet for tourists who flock here in droves in the summer months. At the time of Queen Elizabeth I, however, Studland was famous for quite another reason, for this was the lair of pirates. But before the story of one of them, Roger Munday, and of his brother William, an innkeeper of the village is told, it is necessary to set the scene.

Piracy benefited not only the pirates themselves but also the tradesmen who provided them with victuals; the merchants who purchased their goods, and the vice admirals and customs officials who received bribes for permitting them to ply their trade. Not only that, customs duties were levied on pirated goods, and a further one-tenth of the value of such goods was payable to the Lord High Admiral of England. Also, in times of war, the pirate ships could be mobilised to fight the enemy without imposing any additional burden on the exchequer. In Dorset, the pirates operated, primarily, from West Lulworth and Weymouth/Melcombe Regis.

When Queen Elizabeth I came to the throne in 1558, she found herself under pressure from France, Spain and Scotland (whose merchantmen were under constant threat of attack by English pirates) to suppress piracy. In 1565, Commissioners were appointed and given the task of apprehending the pirates; examining them before a jury of twelve men, and if appropriate, sending them for trial at the Admiralty Sessions. The weakness of this system was that the Commissioners were chosen from local justices and deputy lieutenants, who had a conflict of interest in that they themselves had a vested interest in piracy. Therefore, in 1577, a commission for the 'reformation of piracy' was established, whereby an official from the High Court of the Admiralty would sit with the local commissioners to ensure that they performed their duties satisfactorily. The Commission reported back to the Privy Council – a committee of the Queen's closest advisers – to which it was answerable.

In the following year, 1578, several Dorset pirates were apprehended at sea. Of these, seven were tried; condemned to death and hanged at Wapping, on the banks of the River Thames. In addition, Dorset's Vice Admiral, Sir Richard Rogers of Bryanston, was forced to endure the humiliation of being fined the sum of £100, and was ordered to compensate the original owners of the pirated goods which he had received.

Following this considerable setback, the remaining pirates were obliged to shift the centre of their activities to Studland in the Isle of Purbeck; where they knew that they could rely on the goodwill of Francis Hawley. Hawley was Deputy to Sir Christopher Hatton, who in 1576, had been appointed Constable of Corfe Castle, Lord Lieutenant of the Isle of Purbeck, and also its Vice Admiral (and Guardian of Brownsea Island situated at the mouth of Poole Harbour) by the Queen. The harbour was a place of great importance to the pirates, for they could re-victual their ships and also shelter them there in bad weather.

Hawley's officer/servant at Studland was George Fox, whose duty it was to board all pirated ships which entered Studland Bay, and make an inventory of their goods in order to calculate what custom duty was payable; also to claim his share of those goods on behalf of Hatton, his master.

The principal pirates operating out of Studland Bay in the latter part of the 16th century were Clinton Atkinson, Valentine (alias Baugh) Vaughan, William Arnewood, Thomas Walton (alias Purser,) and John Piers. Their leader was the infamous Stephen Heynes, who once placed a knotted rope around the head of the master of a captured vessel and used it as a tourniquet in order to extract information from him. The pirate chiefs came from such places as London, Cornwall, and elsewhere. None were local men.

Pirated goods were sold to merchants who came from Poole, and from as far afield as Hampshire and the Isle of Wight. The great barn in Studland village served as a repository for such goods. When they were not at sea, the pirates spent their leisure time drinking and playing dice and cards in the inns in Studland at which they lodged. There were three such inns. They belonged, respectively, to Roger Munday, who was also a member of Heynes's ship's company; to his brother William, who was also a fisherman, and to Joan Chaddocks of Corfe Castle. Piracy was a brutal business, both on sea and on land, as this statement by pirate Clinton Atkinson reveals: 'William Munday, his house [inn] is the hell of the world, and he the devil.' One may imagine the pirates, strutting about in the fine clothes – made of satins, velvets and lace, which they had pirated, arguing over games of cards and dice, and engaging in drunken brawls with one another.

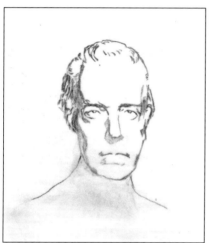

William Vaughan, from a bust by Sir Francis Chantrey.

Even in Studland, remote a place though it was, the pirates and their accomplices were not beyond the reach of the authorities, as was proved on 6 February 1581, when William Munday was called to account. He was examined, on suspicion of being implicated in piracy, by Dr David Lewis, Judge of Her Majesty's High Court of Admiralty, 'Certayne articles [charges, or indictments]' having been brought against him, 'on behalf of Richard Gourneye and company.' (Gourneye, it is assumed, was a French merchant whose ships had been the victim of piracy.)

In his statement to the court, Munday admitted that his wife had received a quantity of flax from the Studland pirates, 'whiche she delyvered to Francys Clerke [presumably meaning Francis Hawley's clerk].' He also stated that Hawley had sent some of the pirated wine which he had seized, to the City of London. Munday also admitted that he had been in the company of the pirates mentioned in the article, 'on lande, and hath eate and drinke with them,' but he could not apprehend them, neither did he dare to do so. He also admitted that his brother Roger, had obtained a, 'pipe [cask] of Canarye wynes [sweet wines from the Canary Islands]' from the pirates, which he sold at his inn, 'whereof this examinante [Munday] and others drancke.'

Munday stated that the previous July (1580), when he was out fishing in his boat, he was summoned by Captain Arnewood who had brought a captured French ship into the bay laden with, 'fish of the bancke' (a reference to the Grand Bank fishing grounds of Newfoundland.) Whereupon, Arnewood unloaded, 'thre hundrethe [hundredweight] or upwards of fish for George Foxe' who was aboard Arnewood's man-of-war at the time. Munday then took the fish ashore where his son Thomas, delivered it to Fox. It was then collected by Francis Hawley. For his trouble, Munday was rewarded with, 'thre cople [six] of fishe' by Arnewood.

On another occasion, about a year previously, said Munday, Captain Arnewood captured a Flemish fly boat (small, swift, square-rigged sailing boat), and Captain Purser and Captain Charles Buctloye captured, 'a prize with wynes.' (The captains and crews of these 'prizes' would either have been killed, or cast adrift in small boats to take their chance on the open sea.)

Munday also stated that George Fox and one of the pirates came aboard Arnewood's ship, from which Fox carried away, 'thre or foure suger [sugar] loaves.' He also said that Thomas Aires [Ayres, one of Hawley's deputies at Corfe Castle,] 'had 2 pipes of Canarye wynes' which were unshipped and taken to his farm barn. In the event, Munday was released without charge. Others were not so fortunate.

In October 1581, Studland pirate John Piers, was betrayed and apprehended by fellow pirate Thomas Walsh. Piers and several of his companions, were tried at Corfe Castle, found guilty, and condemned. In March 1582, they were hanged at Studland Beach in the traditional manner, so that, as the tide came in, their corpses appeared to dance upon the waves. Meanwhile, when the remaining pirates failed to take the hint and cease their nefarious activities, it was inevitable that further setbacks would follow.

In the summer of 1583, the Queen's ships *Bark Talbot* and *Unicorn* captured seven pirate men-of-war, together with three prizes, which they themselves had captured. The outcome was that 43 pirates were examined in the Tower of London by Dr Julius Caesar, Judge of the High Court of Admiralty, and 3 others. The prisoners were all found guilty, but only seven of them, all captains, were condemned to death; the remainder being pardoned. Those hanged at Wapping included Atkinson, Purser, and Vaughan. (Steven Heynes escaped the hangman's noose, having been swept overboard in a storm and drowned the year previously.)

In the autumn of 1583, another nineteen people, all from Purbeck, were sent to London to be examined. They included the Munday brothers, George Fox, and Francis Hawley. In the light of his support for the pirates, Hawley was demoted from being Vice Admiral of Purbeck to being Deputy Vice Admiral. Soon afterwards, however, he obtained the post of Deputy Vice Admiral of Dorset.

For William Munday, this was to be his second examination, and again, it was Dr Lewis who undertook it. This time, it was in respect of Articles given against him on behalf of Peter Bard, Arnold Duverger, and other merchants of Rochelle (La Rochelle – a French sea port on the bay of Biscay), where it was alleged that, 'certayne spoyles [had been] committed bye Clinton Atkinson on their goods.' Munday confirmed that Atkinson and his company had, the previous June, brought two captured French ships into Studland Bay, which were laden, 'with Flaunders commodities of all sortes' (Flanders formerly being a region of north-west Europe), which they, 'made sale of.' Munday also stated that he was commanded by Hawley to accompany him to Atkinson's ship, 'in Studlande Roade' (a 'road' being a safe anchorage) to see who was coming in their boats to buy and carry away, 'those goodes whiche he had.' On that occasion, said Munday, Hawley was presented with three sugar loaves, one or two Spanish 'skynnes' and two pipes of wines with sugar. These 'skynnes' were the hides of bulls, out of which shoes – and in particular ladies' shoes – were made. The hides were, therefore, highly sought after. They originated from Córdoba in Spain, where they were a product of the bull-fighting industry. Munday also asserted that various other people, including John Haywardes, John Prattyn, William Cotton, and Henry Chattocke, all of Studland, had purchased sugar and pipes of wine from Captain Arnewood. He also revealed that his son Thomas was present with Cotton and Chattocke at the time.

William Munday led a charmed life. Twice, he was sent to London to be questioned by the authorities, and twice he was released without being charged. For him, crime paid, as his ownership of 5 acres of arable land and 11 acres of pastureland in Studland indicates.

As for his brother Roger, he also escaped unscathed from his examination of 1583. This was despite his having been a member of pirate leader Steven Heynes' ship's company.

The above events reflected Queen Elizabeth's determination to bear down heavily upon the pirates. She was successful, and the result was that their activities in Studland now came to an end. Nevertheless, the Mundays of Studland continued to live and multiply: the children of William's son Thomas, all being christened in Studland's Church of St Nicholas.

Church of St Nicholas, Studland.

2

Lady Bankes, Defender of Corfe Castle, and her Husband Sir John

The words 'Corfe Castle' can refer either to the castle itself, or to the adjacent village, or to both! The castle is set on a mound, in a natural gap in the northern range of Purbeck Hills which stretch for a distance of 10 miles from Handfast Point in the east, to Worbarrow Bay in the west.

The word 'Corfe' derives from the Anglo-Saxon word 'corf' – meaning to cut. In other words, it refers, in this instance, to a cutting in the hills. In Saxon times (5th – 11th century), before the castle was built, a hunting lodge stood on the site - the surrounding area having been designated as 'The Royal Forest of Purbeck'. Today, people visit Corfe Castle to see the castle itself, which is now a ruin; to visit the National Trust shop and tearooms, and to enjoy the enchanting and unspoilt mediaeval village.

Enough of the castle remains, including much of the great keep, the mighty inner and outer gatehouse, and the surrounding ('curtain') walls, to give an idea of just how magnificent it was in the days of its glory. So how did what was once regarded as an impregnable fortress, come to be a ruin?

For a period of three years during the English Civil War (1642-1651), Mary, Lady Bankes defended Corfe Castle in the heart of Dorset's Isle of Purbeck, for the King, Charles I, against the Parliamentary (rebel) forces of Oliver Cromwell who had laid siege to it.

Corfe Castle's Norman keep, which has stood for over 750 years and is visible from as far away as Poole, 7 miles distant as the crow flies.

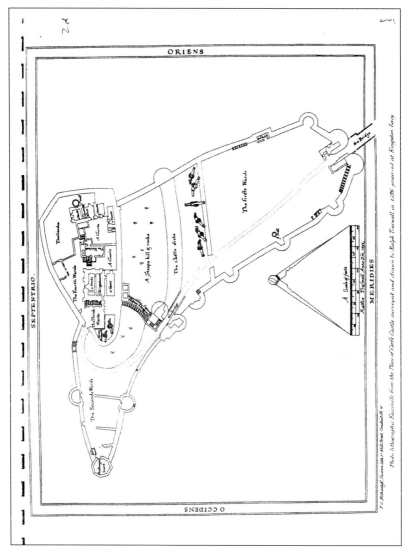

Corfe Castle, by Ralph Treswell, from the Reverend John Hutchins' History of Dorset.

19

The building of Corfe Castle was commenced in the 12th century under King Henry I, and it is a tribute to King Edward I, who rebuilt it in the year 1240, that four hundred years later it was still, to all intents and purposes, impregnable. Furthermore, Lady Bankes was able to mount successful defences of the castle against numerous attacks, and to withstand several sieges with only a small, and sometimes minimal garrison.

Even today, visitors to Corfe Castle can easily see why it was such a formidable stronghold. It stands on a promontory with hills on either side, and is partly surrounded by a deep ditch. It has three, separately defensible 'wards' (or baileys): each surrounded by 'curtain' walls and towers. The entrance to the outer ward consists of a mighty outer gatehouse, complete with arrow loops, a machicolation slot (through which stones or hot embers could be rained down on any attacker), and fighting deck above. The grooves in which the portcullis slid up and down are still clearly visible. In the unlikely event of an enemy penetrating the outer ward, he would then be faced with another, similar, south-west gatehouse, which protected the west ward, to which it was necessary to gain access before the inner ward and keep could be attacked.

King Charles I came to the throne in 1625. In 1628 he accepted the 'Petition of Right', produced by the English Parliament the year previously to seek redress on certain issues – among them taxation, property rights, and habeas corpus. However, the following year he dissolved Parliament and ruled without one for the next eleven years, during which time he condoned the persecution of the Puritans (those who believed that the Church of England needed to be reformed.) He also raised taxes by devious and illegal means, and used the Court of Star Chamber (established in 1487) as a substitute for Parliament. The Court became synonymous with the abuse of power by the King and his circle. This led Oliver Cromwell, the Puritan landowner from Cambridgeshire – who was also a Member of Parliament – to create his Model Army with which to oppose the Monarch.

Sir John Bankes of Kingston Lacy near Wimborne in Dorset, was Lord Chief Justice at the Court of Common Pleas – a division of the King's Court which had jurisdiction over civil matters. He was also a Member of Parliament and one of the King's Privy Councillors. His father, also John, was a Doctor of Divinity. His family derived its wealth from graphite mines which it owned in Cumberland in the northwest of England; the 'lead' being used in the manufacture of pencils. Sir John was a man of honour, as these lines which he wrote, indicate:

Chief Justice Sir John Bankes, by Gilbert Jackson. Photo: The National Trust

When vertue [virtue] and desert [acts or qualities deserving reward] have gone before, prayse [praise] and commendation/reputation ought to follow. It is the just retinue, which attends upon worth, and will not be left behinde. It is the echo to the voice [voice] and rebounds upon it, by a natural resultancie.

In 1635, Sir John purchased Corfe Castle in the heart of the Isle of Purbeck, and he and his wife furnished it lavishly with tapestries, oriental carpets, books and fine furniture. Nonetheless, they continued to use their home at Kingston Lacy as their main residence. So why did he purchase the castle? Perhaps, because he could see that trouble was brewing, and in this, he was quite right.

The Civil War broke out in 1642 when King Charles I raised his standard at Nottingham. He established his Royal capital at Oxford, where he made his home at Christchurch College. Mindful of the need for security, Sir John

Arabella Bankes, Mrs Gilly; by Sir Peter Lely. Photo: The National Trust

promptly moved his family – Lady Bankes and their six sons and four daughters to Corfe Castle, taking care to stock up with a plentiful supply of food and ammunition. Their other two daughters, Mary and Alice, were married and lived in Oxfordshire and Buckinghamshire respectively. In that year, the Bankes's youngest daughter Arabella was born at Corfe Castle.

Soon after the outbreak of hostilities, Sir John was summoned to York, to join King Charles's Privy Council. By failing to oppose the Militia Bill, and thereby offending his sovereign, he demonstrated what his descendant Viola Bankes described as, 'independent judgment, which amounted to stubbornness.' This Bill, which was put forward in December 1641, proposed that the King surrender both his control of the armed forces, and his right to nominate their commanders, and that Parliament should be granted these rights instead. The King refused to give this Bill his assent.

Sir John had good reasons for acting as he did, as a letter, which he wrote to Mr Green, Member of Parliament for Corfe, on the current dispute between Charles and Parliament demonstrates:

I have studied all meanes which way matters may be brought to a good conclusion between the king and the houses [of Parliament], all high wayes of force will be distructive; and if we should have civill warrs, it would make us a miserable people, and might introduce foreign powers; therefore, there is no other way left but the way of accommodatin…'

In other words, Sir John was clearly no warmonger.

In 1643, the rebel forces made their first attempt to take Corfe Castle; choosing a time when Sir John was away in Oxford, having responded to a summons from the King to muster there. The rebel commanders Sir Walter Erie and Sir Thomas Trenchard, had already achieved great success by capturing all the important towns between Poole and Lyme Regis. They chose May Day on which to attack, when they knew that every able-bodied man in Corfe would have left the castle for the countryside, and be engaged in the traditional hunt for a stag. However, they had not counted upon the sterling qualities of Sir John's wife, Lady Bankes, who at the time had only five men whom she could call upon to defend the castle. Her Ladyship, having been forewarned of the rebels' intentions, promptly barred the castle's doors against them. That same month, Sir John returned home for a brief visit; the enemy having presumably left the scene, at least for the time being.

Mary, Lady Bankes; enamel miniature by Henry Bone. Photo: The National Trust

The rebels subsequently demanded that Lady Bankes hand over her four small artillery pieces, and sent forty seamen from Poole in order to try to persuade her to do so. The probable rationale for this was that sailors, being adept at climbing ships' rigging, might therefore be equally adept at scaling the castle's walls! However, this attempt also ended in failure. It was only when the Governor of Wareham ordered that no one be allowed to leave the Castle, and no provisions be allowed into it that Lady Bankes was forced to relent and hand over her cannon. She now requested help from the King's forces, commanded by Prince Maurice and the Marquis of Hertford, who were presently near Blandford. They responded by dispatching a Captain Lawrence of Purbeck and a small contingent of men to reinforce the Castle's woefully small garrison.

A large force of rebel horsemen arrived and began firing their cannon down on the castle from the hilltops on either side. However, their cannon balls made little impression on its strong walls. There were times when the efforts of the attackers slackened, and the defenders were able to replenish their stocks of food and gunpowder. A foraging party even managed to bring eight cows and a bull into the castle. Now, the rebels were to try another tactic altogether.

In June 1643, Sir Walter Erle returned to the fray, together with Captains Sydenham, Jarvis and Skutt, and several hundred soldiers and horsemen. They brought with them a culverin – a cannon, which, with its long barrel, permitted a greater accuracy of fire. In addition, two siege engines were employed which slowly and ominously made their way up the grassy slopes. These became nicknamed the 'great sow' and the 'lesser sow'. According to Dorest historian and antiquarian the Reverend John Hutchins:

> The great sow was 35 foote long and 9 foote broade: it was made upon 4 wheels, made of timbers, bound about with hoopes of iron; their axell trees were one, the rim was great round bars of iron, the beams she was bult [built] upon being of timbar [timber]. Thaie [they] had cross beams to worck with there levars, to forse [force] her along as thaie plesed to guide har. The hinder part of the sow was left open for there [their] men to goe in and outt att. The fore parte of the sow had 4 dowres [doors], 2 in the ruffe [roof] and 2 one in the lower parte, which did hang upon great iron huckes [hooks], but were not open till they came to the wall of the castell [castle], when thaie intended to worck through the castell [walls] with there tooles thaie had provided.... The sow was lickwaies [likewise], covard [covered] ovar with 2 rowes of hides and 2 rowes of sheepe skinnes: soe that noe musket bullet or steele arow could pearse [pierce] it, of which triell [attempt] was often made.

> The lesar [lesser] sow was made only to goe before, to cleere the waie [way], being but 6 foote longe and 3 foote brod [broad], bult strong, as above, only run upon one whele (wheel) lick (like) a wheele barow, and cheefely employd to goe for vitell (provisions) for the great sow to the camp, and for any to com to the bigg sow when thaie desired.

An article in the Royalist newspaper *Mercurius Rusticus* – which, needless to say, was strongly biased in favour of the King – indicates the comical nature of some of the events that took place at Corfe. It was particularly sarcastic about the behaviour of Sir Walter Erle:

> …it was a general observation that valiant Sir Walter [Erle] never willingly exposed himself to any hazard, for being by chance endangered by a bullet shot through his coat, afterwards he put on a beares skinne [bear's skin], and to the eternal honour of this knight's valour, be it recorded, for feare of musquet-shot he was seen to creep on all foure [fours] on the sides of the hill to keep himself out of danger.

The rebels must have entertained high hopes, that with such 'state of the art' war machines, they would soon be able to burrow through the curtain walls. They were disappointed. The defenders fired their muskets at the exposed legs of the attackers, and the latter were able to make no significant headway. Whereupon, the frustrated rebels looted the town.

The rebel Earl of Warwicke, now sent Sir Walter 150 reinforcements, together with scaling-ladders, petards (explosives designed to blow in doors) and grannadoes (small bombs.) However, these men were mainly prisoners and press-ganged sailors with no experience of siege-warfare. Also, it was necessary to ply them with strong drink before they went into action. After six more futile weeks, Sir Walter realised his cause was hopeless and he returned to Poole.

In the autumn of 1643, the Bankes's eldest son, John, now aged 17, became an undergraduate at Oxford University. For some, life went on, regardless of the fact that war was raging! By now, the fortunes of the Royalists had improved to the extent that they had captured several of the south west's major towns, including Weymouth, Exeter, Bristol and Dorchester. Nonetheless, they received a serious setback at Gloucester, where the rebels resisted fiercely, holding up the Royalist army and preventing it from marching on London. In a subsequent encounter near Newbury, the Royalists sustained serious losses.

Meanwhile, at Corfe Castle, the rebels demonstrated their lack of respect for the Parish Church of Saint Edward the Martyr, by stripping lead from its roof to make shot; ripping out the organ pipes, which they used as powder casks, and even stabling their horses in the building and turning the font into a drinking trough.

By the autumn of 1644, when Sir John came home once again for what was to be the last time, Corfe Castle stood alone, being virtually the sole pocket of Royalist resistance between Devon and London, with the exception of Dorset's Portland Castle. As the rebels made steady gains, so the King, who had created his own Parliament at Oxford – so there were now two, the rebel one being in London – now found himself short of money. At Christmas-time, Lady Bankes had another misfortune when her husband Sir John, died whilst at Oxford with the King. Surprisingly, she and her daughters were able to make the journey to that city for the funeral, where they were joined by her sons. Did the rebels allow her safe passage, or did she receive a Royalist escort? Whichever was the case, is not known.

Lady Bankes was a methodical person who kept detailed records of her expenditure in her account book. One such item refers to, 'a neckleace of pearle 2 ropes [strings],' which she had purchased for her daughter Mary for the price of £120. Now it was her unhappy duty to list her late husband's funeral expenses. This included an amount for the coffin of £3.6s.0d.; for mourning apparel for her mother, brother, maidservants, sons, sons-in-law, daughters, and for 'the gentlemen' and for '10 ordinary men' £153, and the tailor's bill for making them, £10.9s.0d. Nonetheless, despite her loss, and despite her continuing predicament, Lady Bankes was not prepared to surrender the castle.

In January 1645, Captain Butler, the Parliamentary Governor of Wareham, rode with his horsemen into Corfe and, having driven the defenders back inside the Castle, plundered and vandalised the town. Still, Lady Bankes did not give in. That October, Colonel Bingham, Parliamentary Governor of Poole, began a new siege of the castle. However, a Royalist force from Oxford – consisting of 120 soldiers under a Captain Cromwell – marched on Wareham. Here, they disguised themselves as rebels, and captured the town's Governor, Captain Butler and two (real) rebels. Then, taking their prisoners with them, they proceeded to Corfe Castle. Lady Bankes was desperately short of provisions. She could not accommodate them, and was therefore obliged to refuse their offer of help and send them on their way. However, she kept the three rebel prisoners as possible future bargaining counters. The King was finally defeated by Cromwell at the Battle of Naseby in June 1645.

Lady Bankes continued her resistance, but the end came in late February 1646, when she was betrayed by two members of her garrison. Captain Lawrence, who had commanded the defenders of the castle in 1643, hatched a plot which enabled the rebel Captain Butler to escape, and Lieutenant Colonel Pitman tricked the Governor of the castle, Colonel Anketil, into giving him permission to go to Somerset, allegedly to fetch reinforcements. Instead, Pitman went to the rebel garrisons at Weymouth and at Lulworth and brought back 140 or so rebel soldiers; 50 of whom were admitted to the castle by its unsuspecting occupants in the early hours of the morning. At a pre-arranged signal, the rebels within, and Colonel Bingham from Poole – who was cognisant of the plot and was without – launched their attack. After a short, but desperate struggle, Lady Bankes was forced to surrender.

Colonel Bingham generously spared the lives of the defenders – of whom there were 140. The rebels now proceeded to loot all the Bankes family's possessions, but, in recognition of Lady Bankes's bravery, Oliver Cromwell made the symbolic gesture of allowing her to keep the keys of the castle. She was also granted a modest allowance on which to live. In March 1646,

Parliament ordered that Corfe Castle be slighted.

Three years later, in January 1649, King Charles I was tried, condemned to death and beheaded. Cromwell declared the establishment of a Commonwealth, with himself as Chairman of its Council of State. The experiment was not a success. Parliament, in which a substantial number of Royalists remained, obstructed his reforms and in 1653, he therefore dissolved it. He ruled briefly as head of a Puritan Convention, and, following the implementation of a new Constitution, as Lord Protector. He dissolved Parliament again in 1655, with a view to establishing regional rule in England under ten major generals. Again, the experiment failed. Cromwell died in 1658 and two years later in 1660, the Monarchy was restored and Charles II came to the throne.

Mindful of the Bankes family's loyalty to his late father during the Civil War, the new King made Sir John and Lady Bankes's son and heir Ralph, a knight and allowed him to recover his estates. (The Bankes's eldest son John had died unmarried, in 1656.)

Lady Bankes died in 1661. The inscription on her tombstone declares that she:

HAD THE HONOUR TO HAVE BORNE
WTH A CONSTANCY AND COURAGE ABOVE HER SEX
A NOBLE PROPORTION OF THE LATE CALAMITIES,
AND THE HAPPINESS TO HAVE OUTLIVED THEM
SO FAR AS TO HAVE SEEN THE RESTITUTION OF THE
GOVERNMENT WITH GREAT PEACE OF MIND....

Sequel
The last owner of Kingston Lacy House was Henry John Ralph Bankes, who died in 1981. He bequeathed his 16,000 acre estate, which included Kingston Lacy House and estate, Studland, Corfe Castle, and its surrounding Purbeck Hills, to the National Trust.

Corfe Castle as it may once have looked.
Photo: Liz Agnew (Proprietor, Corfe Castle Model Village and Gardens)

Some latter-day 'Cavaliers' enjoying Corfe Castle in the more relaxed atmosphere of the 1990s!

3

Benjamin Jesty, Pioneer of Smallpox Vaccination

Dunshay Manor is situated at the end of a leafy lane – about halfway between Swanage and Corfe Castle – in the lee of the southern range of Purbeck Hills which run from Durlston, south of Swanage, to converge with the northern range at Worbarrow Bay. The name 'Dunshay' derives from the Old English word 'dun' – meaning a down – and 'hayes' – meaning an enclosure. Many fascinating characters have lived at Dunshay Manor (which is believed to date from the 9th or 10th century), one of whom was farmer Benjamin Jesty, born in 1737, who became famous, not in the field of agriculture, but in the field of medicine.

Jesty lived and farmed at Yetminster in North Dorset. He possessed a collection of books, and wrote in an elegant hand. For many years, he fulfilled the role of Land Tax Assessor and Collector. Jesty is chiefly remembered, however, as a pioneer of smallpox vaccination.

An entry in the Vestry Minute Book of 1801 ('Vestry' being the administrative committee of the church) indicates that the church authorities were concerned about protecting the inhabitants of the area against the dreaded disease of smallpox: 'Benefit of inoculation to be offered to the poor for 5/- [five shillings,] payable at the rate of 6d [sixpence] per week.'

Swanage had suffered an epidemic of smallpox 40 years earlier in 1761, and

Benjamin Jesty, by Michael W Sharp. By kind permission of
The Wellcome Foundation, Wellcombe Library, London

also in 1762. The disease, caused by a virus, is a highly contagious one, with an incubation period of between one and three weeks. The sufferer experiences a high fever, vomiting, headaches, and generalised aches and pains. Within a few days, a rash appears which spreads to cover the entire body. Within another few days, these spots turn to fluid-filled blisters – or 'vesicles' – which then become filled with a foul-smelling pus. As the fever subsides, crusts form over these pustules, which, when they heal, leave permanent scars known as 'pock marks'. The disease has a high mortality and may leave the sufferer deaf or blind.

A further entry in the Minute Book, this time signed by, 'A Bell, Rector', states, 'That the Vaccine Inoculation be introduced and recommended in the Parish.' In fact, it was the enlightened and energetic Dr Andrew Bell, who would vigorously promote the idea of vaccination in Purbeck. He began by asking Swanage schoolmaster Joseph Gover, whether the parents of his pupils would care to have their offspring vaccinated. The outcome was that during the spring of 1803, Bell, assisted by his wife Agnes, vaccinated in excess of 200 people.

It was inevitable that Bell would come to hear of the exploits of Dorset tenant farmer Benjamin Jesty, who had arrived at Dunshay (situated 3 miles to the west of Swanage) from Yetminster with his wife and family in the year 1797. Jesty too was a smallpox vaccinator, and his story was as follows.

In the autumn of 1771, Jesty's home village of Yetminster was faced with a smallpox epidemic which, in February of the following year, was still raging. This led the Vestry to declare their intention of offering those who so wished it, inoculation against the disease by a 'Surgeon of Eminence', and at the parish's expense. What this meant in practice was that the surgeon in question would take smallpox matter from an infected individual and scratch it into the skin of the person who desired to be inoculated. As live smallpox matter was used, this was a dangerous procedure, with a high mortality.

When, in 1774, smallpox reappeared in the locality – having previously caused the deaths of many villagers – Benjamin Jesty made up his mind to protect his family, but not by the conventional method described above. He would use an altogether different technique.

For those who lived in the country, it was common knowledge that during a smallpox epidemic, no one was guaranteed to be spared from the infection, apart from two groups of people. The first, were those who had suffered smallpox on a previous occasion, survived the attack, and had thereby had become immune. The second, were those who had previously contracted cowpox. (This is because – as is now known – the antibodies produced as the result of an infection with cowpox are equally efficacious against smallpox.) This was a fact that Jesty himself had known since he was a boy.

Cowpox, which is related to smallpox, is a disease of cattle, causing blisters to form on the cows' udders. It is almost inevitable, therefore, that those who milked the cows – a task generally undertaken by milkmaids – would catch cowpox. However, this disease, unlike smallpox, is not a serious one, either for cattle or for human beings. Jesty's milkmaids were Ann Notley and Mary Reade. So confident were they of their immunity to smallpox that they nursed, without fear, relatives of theirs who had contracted the disease.

At the time of the 1774 Yetminster smallpox epidemic, Jesty and his wife Elizabeth had three children: Robert (aged three), Benjamin junior (aged two), and Elizabeth junior (born in the previous year.) Rather than sit back and wait for them to contract smallpox, Jesty decided to take matters into his own hands. He would not consult the medical profession. Instead, he would use a method which he himself had devised; one which he believed was both safe and effective.

When he heard that cowpox had broken out in a herd of cows belonging to a neighbouring farmer, Mr William Elford of Chetnole, Jesty persuaded his wife and their two sons to accompany him to Elford's farm. Having identified a blister on the udder of one of the infected animals, Jesty used a darning needle to lance the blister, and then scratched his wife's forearm and the boys' upper arms with the needle, thereby deliberately infecting them with cowpox. Why did Jesty not inoculate himself also? Because he himself had, 'gone through [caught] the cow-pock [cowpox] many years before.'

As far as the two boys were concerned, the cowpox ran its normal course and they recovered completely. For Jesty's wife, however, it was a different story. Her arm swelled, and she developed a high fever. When the doctor from nearby Cerne Abbas was summoned, he was not unsympathetic to what the Dorset farmer had done in his attempt to safeguard his family. 'You have done a bold thing, Mr Jesty, but I will get you through if I can.' (By bold, the doctor probably meant reckless.) In the event, Elizabeth made a full recovery. The technique used by Jesty subsequently became known as 'vaccination' – from the Latin 'vacca', meaning 'cow'.

Although, for Jesty it was mission accomplished, amongst the villagers of Yetminster there was a great deal of anger and apprehension. According to Mrs William May, a relative of Jesty:

> When the fact became known that he [Jesty] had vaccinated his wife and sons, his friends and neighbours who hitherto had looked up to him with respect on account of his superior intelligence and honourable character, began to regard him as an inhuman brute, who could dare to practise experiments upon his family. The sequel of which would be, as they thought, their [the Jesty family's] metamorphosis into wild beasts. Consequently, the worthy farmer was hooted at, reviled, and pelted whenever he attended the markets in his neighbourhood.

Jesty, however, had no such misgivings about his family turning into cattle. He believed that:

There is little risk in introducing into the human constitution matter from the cow, as we already [and] without danger eat the flesh of and drink the milk, and cover ourselves with the skin of this innocuous animal.

By 1797, the Jestys had produced two more sons and two more daughters. They now relocated to Dunshay Manor near Worth Matravers in Purbeck, where Benjamin managed, as tenant farmer, the adjacent Downshay Farm. By now, people's attitude to vaccination was beginning to change. The medical profession had woken up to the possibilities of vaccination, and only the previous year, Gloucester physician Dr Edward Jenner, had inoculated cowpox matter – not, as Jesty had done, from the cow itself, but from a cowpox vesicle from the hand of an infected dairymaid – into the arm of an eight-year-old boy.

Having heard of Jesty's pioneering work as a smallpox vaccinator, Bell decided that Jesty deserved to be rewarded for his work. Bell, therefore, prepared a paper, dated 1 August 1803, which he sent to the Original Vaccine Pock Institute (founded in December 1799 and run by Dr George Pearson), and also to Member of Parliament for Southampton, George Rose. In it, he proposed that Jesty be recognised as the first vaccinator.

The outcome was that in 1805, Jesty accepted an invitation to visit the Institute in London: a journey which he made with his eldest son Robert (then aged 28.) Here, Jesty was presented with a pair of gold-mounted lancets, the sum of fifteen guineas for his expenses, and a testimonial scroll which read as follows:

As a testimony of our personal regard, and to commemorate a fact as that of preventing the Smallpox by inoculating the Cowpock 31 years ago, at our request a three-quarter length portrait of Mr Jesty is painted by that excellent artist Mr [Michael W] Sharp, to be preserved at the Original Vaccine Pock Institution.

The testimony, dated 6 September 1805, was signed by 3 physicians, 2 consulting surgeons, 2 surgeons, 3 visiting apothecaries, 2 treasurers, and by the Society's Secretary William Sancho.

Despite giving Jesty a warm welcome, it should be noted that the Society's members were somewhat amused by what they considered to be his outmoded attire, and also, doubtless, by his broad Dorset accent. However, he himself, 'did not see why he should dress better in London than in the country.' As for having his portrait painted, Jesty, according to his friend, Swanage clergyman the Reverend JM Colson, found the sittings very tedious, and could only be kept quiet by Mrs Sharp, the artist's wife, playing to him on the pianoforte.

Whilst in London, both Jesty and his son were inoculated with (live) smallpox. Neither suffered any subsequent ill effects, which proved that they were still immune to smallpox from their previous vaccinations with cowpox. Jesty had proved his point beyond all doubt.

Jesty died on 16 April 1816, aged 79. His widow, Elizabeth, died on 8 January 1824, aged 84. The couple are buried in adjacent graves in the churchyard of Worth Matravers' Parish Church of St Nicholas of Myra.

Sequel

Despite the efforts of those such as Benjamin Jesty, Dr Andrew Bell and Dr Edward Jenner, smallpox continued to be a scourge of mankind, killing, in the 20th century alone, an estimated 300-500 million people. However, a concerted effort at vaccination enabled the World Health Organisation (the United Nations Organisation's public health arm) to declare, in the year 1979, that smallpox has now been completely eradicated throughout the world.

4

Dr Andrew Bell, Clergyman, Educationalist and Social Reformer

The popular seaside resort of Swanage may be approached by road, by pleasure boat from Bournemouth or Poole, or by steam train from Corfe Castle. On the north side of Swanage Bay lies Handfast Point, and on the south side, Durlston Head. Here, in the early 19th century, lived one of the greatest educationalists of the day.

Andrew Bell was born on 27 March 1753 at the university city of St Andrews, Scotland. His father was a perruquier (wig-maker). Having graduated from the university in mathematics, philosophy, metaphysics and classics, he became tutor to the sons of Mr Braxton, a wealthy tobacco planter in Virginia, USA.

In 1784, having returned to St Andrews, Dr Bell entered the priesthood and became Curate of the Episcopal Chapel of Leith – a district on the north side of the City of Edinburgh.

Dr Andrew Bell, by Charles Turner.

In February 1787 he set sail for India; there to deliver a series of lectures on natural philosophy. On his arrival at Madras, he was offered the post of Superintendent to the East India Company's 'Military Male Orphan Asylum', which was currently under construction. This was an institution for the education of orphans, and also for the illegitimate sons of native women and British soldiers.

Whilst he waited for the asylum to be completed, Bell took the post of Chaplain to Fort St George, and also to various regiments of the British army. (Built by the East India Company in 1639, Fort St George was the first British fortress in India.) He also delivered his lectures, as intended, and was the first person to introduce the hot-air balloon and ice to the Indian subcontinent.

It was at the asylum that Bell developed his legendary 'Madras System' of teaching. This operated as follows. Faced with a shortage of teachers, he made the brighter pupils of each class 'tutors' to the less bright ones, and was able to say, in May 1792, that, 'every boy is either a master or a scholar and generally both. He teaches one boy, while another teaches him.' Also, by paying the senior boys or 'monitors' a small salary, this had the added advantage of saving the asylum's directors a considerable sum of money in teachers' salaries. Other features of the 'Madras System' were that pupils were streamed, according to ability rather than by age, and were encouraged to think for themselves, rather than to learn by rote. Also, a system of rewards in the form of book prizes and medals, was preferred to corporal punishment.

Ill health forced Bell to leave India in August 1796. He was now a wealthy man, having made a fortune from investments, and also being in receipt of an East India Company pension. He returned to the United Kingdom, where he wrote a report on his new System, in the hope that it would be widely adopted throughout the land. In this, he was not disappointed. The 'Madras System' spread, not only throughout England, but also to Wales and Ireland, and as far afield as the British colony of Barbados.

Meanwhile, back in England, Joseph Lancaster, son of a Southwark shopkeeper and a Quaker, had come, independently, to the same conclusions as Bell, and in 1798, had founded an elementary school in Borough Road, Southwark, based on the monitorial system. Lancaster and Bell would become bitter rivals.

Bell settled, for a time, in Windermere in the English Lake District, where, as Rector, he promoted his 'Madras System' of education. In 1800 he married Agnes Barclay, the daughter of a Church of Scotland minister. In 1801, Bell and his wife moved to Swanage, where he became rector of the town. In this capacity, he displayed his characteristic energy and enthusiasm: being described by one of his parishioners as, 'a vigorous revolutionary… [who made] no vague, shadowy statements of abstract doctrines, but attacked Satan wherever he found him.' He also showed his concern for his parishioners, in particular, those who were underprivileged, by assiduously visiting the sick, and supporting the friendly societies (which provided members – who paid a regular subscription – an allowance if they fell ill or had an accident, and also provided them with the services of a doctor, free of charge).

In the late 18th century, educational provision for children was patchy, and also discriminatory against the poor. 'Dame' schools existed throughout the country, and a handful of these, undoubtedly, existed in Swanage. They were established by widows, anxious to earn a little money, who would each set aside a room of their cottage for the purpose. The pupils were the children of farmers and quarry owners – the labouring classes being too poor to afford the fees. Through lack of space, the number of pupils in attendance at each one was, therefore, not more than ten, or so. The level of education received depended, in turn, on the level of education of the widow, her aptitude and willingness to teach. At worst, they were little more than crèches. Aside from this, the main source of education was the Sunday School.

Sunday Schools for Anglicans (members of the Church of England) were established from the late 18th century. The Parish of Swanage had two such Sunday Schools - each with its own schoolmaster. Here, children between the ages of 5 and 14 were taught in the mornings, prior to Matins, and in the afternoons, prior to Evensong (which they were also required to attend!). In the mornings, the children were instructed in stories from the *Holy Bible*, and also in the Liturgy and the Catechism of the Established Church. In the afternoons, such subjects as mathematics, geography and needlework were taught. (Methodists – 'Wesleyans', and Baptists attended separate Sunday Schools.)

Bell was quick to introduce his 'Madras System' into the Sunday Schools, and also to encourage the creation of other schools in the area. As a result, by 1807, the number of Sunday Schools had risen to three, and thirteen new day schools (i.e. non-boarding), also modelled on the 'Madras System', had been created in the parish.

As local historian WM Hardy remarked, in the early 1800s there was, 'little for the young women and maidens to do except knitting, picking up stones in the fields and harvesting….' Bell set about rectifying the situation by introducing straw-plaiting to Swanage, with the objective of establishing a cottage industry for the manufacture of hats, poke bonnets (so called because their brims projected in front,) and baskets.

The two daughters of a Mr Cole, a Swanage stone merchant, commenced operations by making bonnets. It was subsequently agreed, that local children could be admitted to a 'school' to be established at the Cole's home, for a payment of sixpence per week. Initially, twelve children were taught in the mornings according to Dr Bell's 'Madras System'; the afternoons being devoted to straw-plaiting. In order to place the enterprise on a more professional footing, the Cole sisters were sent to Wyke, near Weymouth, to receive proper instruction in the craft. Top quality straw was obtained from London, and a special machine purchased with which to split it. Once split, the straw was flattened using a hand-held tool made of ivory, with a pointed end and grooved along its length.

The number of pupils at the 'school' soon increased to 90, and from here, straw-plaiting spread to the cottages, providing employment for the women of the town. Bell himself, helped to make straw hats fashionable by wearing one himself – locally made, of course! As many as 4,000 bonnets were produced annually and sold, not only locally, but in the surrounding towns, and even as far afield as the Isle of Wight and Devonshire. Latterly, the bonnets were collected from Swanage and District by millinery wholesalers who paid the women according to the quality of their work, and dictated what pattern and style of bonnet was to be produced.

Bell was also passionately concerned with the protection of the population against smallpox – an aim which he had in common with Dorset farmer Benjamin Jesty, about whom more will be said shortly.

Elizabeth Webber, wearing locally made straw-plaited bonnet, and her daughter Elizabeth Ann. Photo: RJ Saville

A favourite pastime of Bell's was to visit his neighbour Thomas Manwell, born in 1751 and therefore two years his senior. Manwell lived across the road from Bell's home, Swanage Rectory, which was situated at the foot of Church Hill. Manwell's father, Joseph, was a carpenter.

Although Manwell was, like his brothers, originally apprenticed to be a quarryman, his father, perceiving him to be, 'of a delicate constitution', supplied him, when he was aged 14, with a small collection of books with which he educated himself in the theory of navigation. For this reason, he was appointed midshipman, under the Lieutenant of Signals at Round Down. Here, a lookout post had been established at the turn of the 18th/19th centuries to give warning of an enemy landing by French Emperor Napoleon Bonaparte. According to poet and writer Robert Southey, 'the solitude of this place was well suited to his habits and feelings, and gave him an opportunity of following his favourite studies.' These were in the fields of astronomy, history, the arts, and the sciences - subjects upon which he conversed with his younger brothers George and Joseph (junior), and doubtless too, with Dr Bell.

A measure of the closeness which Bell felt to Manwell is indicated by the fact that when Manwell died in 1822, the former Rector wrote this epitaph for his tombstone:

Near this stone lie the earthly remains of Mr. Thomas Manwell who (unassisted by education) by the strength of superior genius, and [with] Nature for his guide, broke thro' the barrier to literature, and acquired a degree of knowledge which might have ranked him with the first Philosophers of the Age; but being a child of solitude, his retired meditations were far dearer to him than the requirement of Fame, and if Charity, Humility, and Meekness, with Faith in a Redeemer, be Christianity, he was a perfect Christian.

In 1808, Bell published, 'A Sketch of a National Institution for Training up the Children of the Poor in Moral and Religious Principles and Habits of Useful Industry.' This document led, in 1811, to the creation of the voluntary 'National Society for Promoting the Education of the Poor in the Principles of the Established Church throughout England and Wales,' whose President was the Archbishop of Canterbury. (Prior to this date, the government had been reluctant to finance a national education scheme, and therefore illiteracy was rife. Now, the State would assist the Society by making grants towards teachers' salaries and also towards classroom equipment.)

In 1809, Bell, who by now was separated from his wife, left Swanage for London, then Durham, and finally, Cheltenham in Gloucestershire. A measure of the town's appreciation of him was expressed by the changing of the name of 'Scrap Street', Herston, Swanage to 'Bell Street'. Bell went on to promote his 'Madras System' throughout the country, especially to the south and west of England, and also to Ireland and Wales. In 1813, his chief occupation was that of General Inspector of all of his schools, of which there were now 230 – a number which would more than double over the course of the next three years.

Bell died on 27 January 1832, aged 78. He was buried in Westminster Abbey. At the time of his death the 'Madras System' was established in over 12,000 schools, not only in the United Kingdom and Ireland, but also in British colonies throughout the world.

In his will, Bell left in excess of £120,000, to various organisations, including the Royal Naval School, Greenwich. A large portion of this money would go towards establishing the 'Madras System' in his native land of Scotland, where, in the town of his birth, St Andrews, the Madras College was founded, and in the neighbouring town of Cupar, the Madras Academy. Madras schools were also founded in Edinburgh (including Leith), Glasgow and Inverness. Bell also left a bequest to the Theological Institute of the Scottish Episcopal Church.

Sequel

On 8 August 1833, Princess (later Queen) Victoria visited Swanage and stayed for one night at the Manor House Hotel near to the seafront. It was decided that she, and the Duchess of Kent who was accompanying her, should each be presented with a straw bonnet – one of which had been made at Swanage, and the other at Langton Matravers. The Swanage bonnet was made by Mrs Shorey whose straw millinery shop was adjacent to the hotel. The occasion was somewhat marred by the Rector of Swanage dwelling overlong on his speech, at which the young Princess is said to have become impatient! Sadly, straw-plaited bonnets became unfashionable at the turn of the 19/20th centuries.

Princess Victoria became Queen in 1837. In 1842, an Act of Parliament was passed, 'to afford further facilities for the conveyance and endowment of sites for schools.' This paved the way for the creation of 'National Schools' – each to be run in accordance with the tenets of the 'National Society for Promoting the Education of the Poor.' Swanage's National School was built in 1857.

The passing of the 1870 Education Act enabled board schools – under the control of a locally elected board of governors – to be created. In 1880, the Elementary Education Act was passed, requiring all children to attend school until the age of 10 (increased to 12 in 1890.) In 1897, a new school was opened at Mount Scar on the south side of the town, at a cost of £6,000. However, under the 1902 Education Act, both National and Board schools were abolished, and primary and secondary education became the responsibility of the County Council.

In the late 19th and early 20th centuries, a dozen or more private schools opened in the area: the Victorians believing that exposure to the ozone (a molecule containing three oxygen atoms), which was to be found in seaside air was beneficial to health. (Ozone is now considered to be harmful to health!)

5

William Pike and Benjamin Fayle, Suppliers of Clay to Josiah Wedgwood and The Potteries

The area to the south-west of the main road from Wareham to Corfe Castle consists of woodland and heathland which is largely undisturbed. However, in the 19th century, it was a hive of activity. This was largely due to the efforts of three men: the brothers John and William Pike from Devonshire, and Benjamin Fayle from London. They, more than any others, were responsible for the development of the Purbeck clay-mining industry.

The discovery of pre-Roman pottery kilns at Shipstal Point in Purbeck, and at other sites along the southern shoreline of Poole Harbour, suggest that clay was mined locally in the Iron Age period (from about 750 BC to 43 AD.) There is also evidence that the Durotriges – a people who inhabited Dorset during the Iron Age – continued to make their distinctive, black-burnished pottery there, even after the Roman occupation which began in 43 AD. The advantage of such sites is obvious. They were within easy reach of the clay pits, and from them, fired products could be transported across the water to Poole. Subsequent generations were to take advantage of this fact, as will shortly be seen.

From the 16th century, various families rented land from Purbeck landowners such as John Calcraft of Rempstone, in order to extract clay. Notable families were those of Brown, Hyde, and Garland. However, these families were overshadowed in the late 18th and early 19th centuries by Messieurs Pike and Fayle.

In Purbeck, clay occurs in lens-shaped deposits which may occupy several acres in area and be up to 50 feet in depth. These lenses may not run horizontally; so what begins as an open-cast pit may end up as an underground mine, if all the clay is to be extracted. (Most clay mines were between 50-100 feet deep, and were rarely deeper than 200 feet.)

Purbeck clay – known as 'ball clay' – is derived from West Country granite. It is highly sought after, even to this day, because of the small and uniform size of its grains. This means that when mixed with china clay (a fine, white clay used in the making of ceramics), it gives the finished china-ware product an added plasticity and strength. It also has the advantage of turning white when fired, and for these reasons, Purbeck clay became known as 'the bones of all earthenware.'

There were two principal reasons for the rapid expansion of the Purbeck clay-mining industry. The first was the introduction of tobacco into England in the mid-1560s, and its subsequent popularisation by English courtier Sir Walter Raleigh – hence a sudden and universal demand for clay pipes. The second, was the introduction, in 1657, of tea to Britain from China – hence the demand for 'china' crockery, which fast began to replace existing wood or pewter vessels and plates in the home. In consequence, the pottery towns of the English Midlands – known as 'The Potteries' – in particular, underwent rapid expansion.

It was at the suggestion of the renowned Staffordshire potter Josiah Wedgwood, that William Pike – born in 1761 – travelled from Chudleigh in Devonshire to Purbeck, with the object of prospecting for Purbeck clay. William's older brother John, remained in Chudleigh where he assisted his father Joseph, who owned a number of trading ships including a 93-ton clay-carrying brigantine. Ball clay was to be found locally in Devonshire's

Bovey Basin bordering the River Teign, and in the last half of 1788, for example, over 1,200 tons of it were shipped by Joseph Pike from the Devonshire port of Teignmouth.

In 1789, William Pike took up residence at Market Place, Corfe Castle in company with a writing clerk (who was paid 12 shillings a week,) a woman servant, and three clay cutters; all of whom he had brought with him from Devonshire. They now proceeded to extract clay from nearby Furzebrook by the following method. First, the vegetation and topsoil were removed. Then, the clay was dug with a long, narrow spade called a 'tubal', and as the working went deeper, stepped sides were created for ease of working.

The clay was then transported laboriously, over the heath to Ridge Wharf near Wareham – first by donkeys fitted with saddlebags, and later by horse-drawn wagon. Here, it was left to weather for a month or two, before being

Josiah Wedgwood. Photo: The Wedgwood Museum Trust, Barlaston, Staffordshire

Opposite page: *Clay-carrying Barges at Ridge Wharf, River Frome, Wareham.* Photo: David Haysom Collection

transported by rowing boat (and later by sailing-barge) down the River Frome and Wareham Channel to Poole. It was now transferred to larger, sea-going ships for the voyage to Liverpool's River Mersey, and from there by packhorse, or later via the Grand Trunk Canal, to the Staffordshire potteries (commonly known, simply, as 'The Potteries'), or, again by canal, to potteries in London, or at Queenborough in Kent. From such modest beginnings, Pike went on to found, with his brother John, the firm of 'Pike Brothers' and soon, clay was being extracted from an ever-increasing number of opencast pits scattered over an area of many square miles.

In 1791, Pike undertook, over the next five years, to supply Wedgwood with 1,200 tons of clay annually, from pits which he leased from John Calcraft. For this, Pike would receive the sum of £120 per quarter, and an extra 1 shilling and 6 pence for each ton in excess of the agreed amount. (There was a precedent for this, in that Wedgwood had previously been supplied from pits in Stoborough, leased by Thomas Bartlett of Wareham, and from Thomas Hyde of Poole, who leased land near Corfe, also from Calcraft.)

Josiah Wedgwood had achieved international recognition by supplying Empress Catherine the Great of Russia, in 1774, with a 952-piece dinner service of 'Queen's Ware (cream coloured earthenware.) Each and every piece was decorated with one, or more, individually hand-painted scenes featuring the landscape of the British Isles (1244 scenes in all) and each bore the emblem of a green frog within a shield. Why a frog? This was because the palace near St Petersburg, for which the

'Queen's Ware' plate with central, hand-painted view of Castle Acre, Norfolk, and frog crest. Photo: The Wedgwood Museum Trust, Barlaston, Staffordshire

service was intended, stood on marshy ground, and was consequently nicknamed 'The Froggery'!

The Pikes' connection to the Staffordshire potteries was not simply a commercial one. In about 1804, William Pike married Ann Warburton, daughter of a potter from Cobridge, Staffordshire. Subsequently, William and Ann's son John William Pike (born 1814), married Mary Mayer (born 1827), daughter of Thomas Mayer, potter of Longport, Staffordshire and his wife Charlotte.

In 1813, William and Ann Pike – who had seven children in all – acquired Bucknowle House, situated on the edge of Corfe Common near Church Knowle. In about 1815, 'Pike Brothers' commenced mining in the Creech area to the west of Corfe Castle.

Pike had a rival in Benjamin Fayle, a clay merchant and insurance broker of Lombard Street, London. His company, Benjamin Fayle & Co. Ltd., had owned clay pits in the Norden area near Corfe Castle since 1795. In 1806, Fayle had revolutionised the system for transporting clay, by building a 'plateway' 3½ miles in length from his Norden clay pits to Middlebere Creek. The metal tram plates (rails) which were not flanged, were 3 feet in length and ran on the outside of the L-shaped plates. Where one rail abutted onto another, a metal spike held the plates together. This spike was driven into an oak plug, which in turn nestled snugly in the hole bored into its foundation – a large stone, of which there was one on either side of the track. The gauge was 3 feet 9½ ins, and along the plateway, a team of three horses hauled five wagons, each carrying 2 tons of clay.

Not to be outdone, Pikes eventually employed a tramway of their own, which ran in a straight line, the 2 miles from Furzebrook to Ridge Wharf on the River Frome. Its wagons were also hauled by horses. It had the advantage that it was largely gravity assisted. As Pikes expanded their operations westwards, this line was linked to clay pits at Creech, Cotness,

Clay pit at Norden, belonging to Benjamin Fayle. Photo: William Stockley

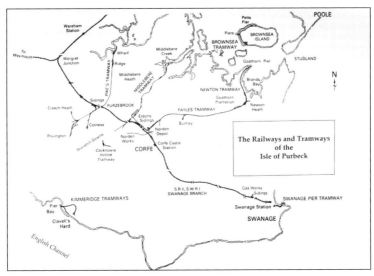

Illustration: The Oakwood Press

Greenspecks and Povington. (The Ridge tramway was built by Watts, Hatherley & Burn of Newton Abbot, who dug clay at Furzebrook. One of their pits subsequently became known as the Blue Pool.)

Sequel

With the death of William Pike in 1833, his sons William Joseph and John William took over the running of the company. In 1851, the Pike and Fayle companies came together briefly at London's Great Exhibition, held at the Crystal Palace (together with Whiteway, Watts & Co., also of Purbeck), to display and sell their clay.

In 1861, John William Pike was living with his wife Mary and family at Wareham, in Westport House, a 'handsome, commodious mansion' which he built for himself. (This was on the site of an army barracks which had been demolished at the conclusion of the Napoleonic Wars in 1815.) In 1867, the Pike family home, Bucknowle House, was demolished and another property built on virtually the same site.

Perhaps the most flamboyant member of the Pike family was John William Pike's son Warburton Mayer Pike. Born on 25 September 1861, Warburton was unfortunate in that his mother Mary Pike, died when he was only 5 years old, and his father John William Pike, died three years later. He and his siblings were, therefore, entrusted to the care of a guardian, and brought up by a governess.

Warburton was educated at Rugby School and Brasenose College, Oxford. From 1884, he made periodic visits to British Columbia (BC), where he explored that province of Canada. He travelled vast distances overland and by canoe – hunting, living off the land, and suffering, on occasion, from frostbite and starvation. In August 1889, he was determined to, 'penetrate this unknown land' north of the Great Slave Lake, in order:

…to see the musk ox, and find out as much as I could about their habits, and the habits of the Indians who go in pursuit of them every year.

Warburton, who was elected a member of the Royal Geographical Society, recounted his adventures in *The Barren Ground of Northern Canada* (1892) and *Through the Sub-Arctic Forest* (1896). He tried his hand at gold prospecting and mining, and he also became provisional director of the Cassiar Central Railway Company. Sadly, however, none of his business ventures were successful.

Warburton donated land on Mayne Island (off BC's south-west coast) for the building of its Church of St Mary Magdalene. Also, the highest hill on Saturna Island (between BC and Vancouver Island,) where he once owned property, is named after him. His life was to end tragically, but not in the dangerous hinterland of British Columbia. In 1915, he returned to England, anxious to play his part for his country in World War I. However, he was now aged 54, and the recruiting office in Bournemouth – where he applied to join the armed forces – rejected him. On leaving the office, he strode down to the seashore, entered the water, and fatally stabbed himself in the heart.

In 1866, the Pike's Tramway lines to Ridge Wharf were replaced by a railway track, with locomotives replacing the horses. The first of these was 'Primus', to be followed later by 'Secundus', 'Tertius' and so forth over the years, right up to 'Septimus'.

***

Although Benjamin Fayle died in 1831, his company, Benjamin Fayle & Co., lived on. In 1860, Fayles commenced clay mining at Newton – the clay being transported by tramway to Goathorn Pier, 2½ miles away. In about 1905, this Newton Tramway was linked to Fayle's Norden works by Fayle's Tramway. Five and three-quarter miles in length, and of 3ft 9in gauge, it ran on conventional railway tracks. The line was subsequently

Fayle's locomotive 'Thames', leaving Corfe Castle for Goathorn, and the consecration of its Mission Church, 26 February 1920. Photo: David Haysom Collection

worked by two steam locomotives. 'Tiny', and the more powerful 'Thames' (which was purchased from the London County Council in 1909).

Fayle's Tramway had the advantage that it was more convenient than the other clay embarkation points on the southern side of Poole Harbour, being situated a mere 2 miles distance from Poole. With the opening of this tramway, the Middlebere Plateway was dispensed with.

The school, which had previously been built at Newton for the benefit of the clay miners' children, closed in 1920. Between 1934 and 1937, an extra 'carriage' (a converted clay wagon,) complete with corrugated iron roof, was added to the clay train, so that the children could be transported to the school at Corfe Castle instead. The sight of the little locomotive puffing its way across the purple, heathery moorland with its clay wagons and a carriage-load of excitable young charges, must have been one to behold!

In 1949, rivalry between the two companies of Pike and Fayle ceased, when they merged under the new name of 'Pike Brothers, Fayle and Company Ltd.' In 1948, the tracks were renewed in order that diesel locomotives could work the line. Finally, in 1970, the tramway, which found itself unable to compete with road transportation, was closed and the tracks were taken up the following year.

In the 1950s, the company was acquired by ECC (English China Clays) Ball Clays Ltd. Clay continues to be extracted from the Purbecks today by ECC plc, which is now owned by the French company Imerys SA.

What remains today of the original clay workings? It was a tradition amongst the miners of old, that when a pit was exhausted and water had accumulated in it, the newest boy-recruit would be sent out to plant it with water lilies. As a result of such foresight, Purbeck is now dotted with idyllic-looking, lily-covered lakes for succeeding generations to enjoy.

As for the Pike family – generations of whom were baptised at the Church of St Peter, Church Knowle, (not far from the site of William Pike's former home, Bucknowle House) – several of its members are buried in the north-east corner of the churchyard.

The Blue Pool at Furzebrook – now a tourist attraction with tea rooms and a museum of the clay industry – was once an opencast clay mine, dug from about 1845 onwards. The pool is remarkable, in that the hue of its water changes with every variation of sunshine, cloud, and even of rain. At one moment, it might be blue, and at another, a rich turquoise, sapphire, or green. It is, therefore, a magnet, not only for tourists, but also for artists and photographers.

6

Charles Hayward, Churchwarden and Smuggler

The village of Langton Matravers in Purbeck consists mainly of one long street of stone-built dwellings. The parish dates from pre-Saxon times, its principal industries being farming and the mining and fashioning of the local Purbeck limestone.

Charles Hayward, born in 1796, was Sexton, Churchwarden and latterly, Rector's Warden of St George's Church, Langton Matravers – a village situated a mile from the sea and near to the coastal town of Swanage. However, his outwardly respectable appearance disguised a dark secret. What kind of environment did he grow up in?

Because of its proximity to France, the coast of southern England has, from time immemorial, been a favourite haunt of smugglers, and this was particularly the case in the 18th and early 19th centuries. Charles Hayward, was not only a smuggler, he was also an established pillar of society. Before his story is told, however, it is important to examine the background to what was an important part of the country's economy.

The aim of the smuggler was to purchase a commodity in France – where the price compared most favourably with that for which it could be bought in England – and then to sell it in England at a price – which allowed him a reasonable profit – but at the same time undercut that of the legally imported commodity. For example, where a keg of brandy could be

Charles Hayward. Photo: Langton Matravers
Local History and Preservation Society

purchased in France for 16/- (shillings), this same keg could be sold in England for £1.2s.6d. (one pound, two shillings and sixpence), which was still 10/- cheaper than brandy purchased legally after excise duty had been paid. The operation was performed on such a scale, that the contraband was stored in dedicated warehouses at French ports such as Roscoff, Cherbourg, Le Havre and Dieppe, prior to shipment.

For its part, the Government, for whom duty on imported goods was an important source of revenue, was anxious to stamp smuggling out. This was particularly the case both prior to, and during the Napoleonic Wars of 1803-1815 (to finance them) and afterwards (to replenish the exchequer).

The Preventive Service – established in 1698 – appointed riding officers to foil the smugglers, who were evading duty on wool being not imported, but EXPORTED from England to the Continent. Each officer was issued with a sword and a pistol, but he had to provide his own horse and was responsible for patrolling a given stretch of coastline. To expect one man to combat a well-organised and determined gang of armed smugglers operating at night, in terrain which they knew like the back of their hands, was quite unrealistic. The cliffs were treacherous; the landing places remote, and the hiding places – often murky quarries with deep caves – plentiful.

From 1713, when it became clear that riding officers alone were ineffectual in their task, dragoons (mounted infantrymen armed with carbines) were made available to back them up, the idea being that they could reach the scene rapidly on horseback. However, by the time they had made the journey from their barracks – which was often some distance inland – the nifty smugglers would, as likely as not, have stashed their goods and left the scene. In 1759, the Government decided that prevention was better than cure, and detailed Royal Naval cutters to patrol the coastline.

In 1822, the Coastguard Service was established; its task being to patrol the shoreline, gather information, and liase with the revenue cutters (small, fast sailing ships.) Each coastguard was issued with a spyglass, together with an early version of the shooting stick, and, in 1829, a musket.

Just how widespread smuggling was, is indicated by the fact that in the early 1820s and 1830s, the majority of the inmates of Dorchester (Dorset's county town) Prison were smugglers, for, as the Prison Register shows, this class of convict outnumbered all the 'Vagrants,' 'Thieves,' and 'Bastardisers' put together. In this, Langton Matravers in Purbeck was represented, as were the coastal villages of Portesham, Preston, Ringstead, and Abbotsbury, to name but a few. The vast majority of the smugglers, however, came from the Isle of Portland.

The prison also contained convicted smugglers from places far inland, such as Tolpuddle, Winfrith, Bere Regis and the Blackmoor Vale, which, presumably, were staging posts where the convoys of pack horses, heavily laden with contraband, paused for rest and refreshment before resuming their journey to places where they could market their ill-gotten gains.

The Prison Register also indicates that, for those smugglers who were caught, the penalties were harsh. For example, a typical entry reads:
1827 Feb. 22. John Gibbs, 20, Portland, Fisherman, Single, Smuggling. Imprisonment until he pays £100.

French smugglers also languished in Dorchester Prison:
June 3 1828, Eugene Bastieu, Cherbourgh [Cherbourg], 36, married. Mar 25 1831, Auguste Josselin, 21, Cherbourgh, France, mariner, married.

Again, each man was imprisoned until he paid the penalty of £100. As for those who had offered violence against the instruments of authority, they were likely to be hanged.

Frenchmen often arrived at the prison in groups of four or five, indicating that they were probably the crews of small boats which had been intercepted by revenue cutters.

With the drastic reduction in import duties by Robert Peel's government in the early 1840s, smuggling became less worthwhile and thereafter, it rapidly declined.

***

Charles Hayward, the smuggler in question, lived at Fig Tree Cottage, Langton Matravers. He followed family tradition and became a quarryman. In 1818, he married Rose Brownsea, and the couple had five children: a boy and four girls. By 1846, when he became Parish Clerk, Hayward was a successful businessman who rented Dancing Ledge quarry (on the coast, one mile to the south of Langton Matravers) from a Mrs Frances Serrell of Durnford Hall. This elegant but eccentric lady fell out with her local parson, the Reverend EF Trotman, and held rival church services in the village, engaging a noisy brass band to drown out the sound of the church choir! In 1860, Hayward was appointed Langton Matravers's first sub-postmaster, whereupon he converted part of his house into a Post Office.

Frances Serrell at her home, Durnford House. Photo: Langton Matravers Local History and Preservation Society

A clue that Hayward was leading a double life is contained in the reminiscences of CWT Dean –

'Charlie' – his elder grandson. Dean was the son of Hayward's youngest daughter Sarah, and her husband William Dean, who had been appointed butler to Frances Serrell when she became a widow. In his reminiscences, Dean recorded an event which occurred on 23 October 1869, when Hayward asked him to assist in a 'business matter'. Wrote Charlie:

> Just after dusk, I was requested by my grandfather to stand outside the church gate – but not to look too involved with anything particular, and I must needs walk to and fro past the gate, and not stand too still. I found this nothing but necessary, since there was a cold wind. My grandfather also gave me strict instructions to alert him – he being within the church – if a Peeler-Policeman came up or down the road. Seven gentlemen arrived variously to meet my grandfather, and they all went inside the church. A Peeler [archaic slang for a police officer, Sir Robert Peel being the man who, as Home Secretary, created the modern London police force] came down the road from Garfield, past me, and thence on to Stepps [Steppes]. I had given the alert (taking my cap off, shaking it, and putting it on again) and whilst the Peeler walked by all was silent in the church, nor any light. Presently came two stone-carts from Garfield end, and the seven gentlemen came out and assisted the drivers with unloading the stones; these were stacked flat-down and not up-down. The men then brought in barrels of all sizes and different shapes. All together

Charles Hayward's grandson, CWT Dean.
Photo: Langton Matravers Local History and Preservation Society

A horse-drawn stone wagon in Langton Matravers's main street in about 1895. Its driver Alfred Masters, having paused at the inn – presumably for refreshment – is now ready to resume his journey! Photo: David Haysom Collection

this went into the church – I could not see where…

Charlie Dean's reminiscences prove beyond doubt that Hayward, outwardly the pillar of respectability was, in fact, a smuggler. Dean then mentioned hearing someone mutter an oath, after accidentally bumping against one of the church bells, which suggests strongly that the 'seven gentlemen' had hidden the barrels in the church's roof.

The contraband had probably been stored at Hayward's quarry, Dancing Ledge, which, because of its remoteness, was the perfect place to land and hide smuggled goods. And what better way of transporting the barrels than to hide them in a waggon under a ton or two of stone. (It is even rumoured that Hayward was not averse to using a hearse for the same purpose!)

In his smuggling activities, Hayward had a great advantage. His eldest daughter Mary had married Thomas Trupp (pronounced 'Troup'), an exciseman who was both a drunkard and a bigamist. Hayward may not have discouraged her in this – having a spy in the 'enemy camp' would undoubtedly have proved useful to him, and Mary would hardly have thanked Trupp had he betrayed his own father-in-law to the Customs and Excise! Also Hayward, having access to unlimited supplies of wines and spirits, may have made sure that in any event, Trupp was too drunk to fulfill his duties.

Mary Trupp was to have an unpleasant shock when the first Mrs Trupp arrived on her doorstep one day, together with five of her and her husband

Mary Trupp (née Hayward).
Photo: Langton Matravers Local History and Preservation Society

Thomas Trupp, drunkard and bigamist.
Photo: Langton Matravers Local History and Preservation Society

Thomas's children. She was indignant, not only that Trupp had married for a second time, bigamously, but also that he had failed to pay maintenance for his children.

As for Frances Serrell, it seems unlikely that she was entirely ignorant of Hayward's smuggling activities. After all, not only was he a tenant of hers, but, as already mentioned, her butler had married his youngest daughter. Further evidence to suggest that Frances Serrell was not all that she might have been comes with the discovery of a concealed passageway linking the attics of two cottages which she owned; also, of a muzzle-loading shotgun in the chimney of a third, next door.

The smuggling activities of Hayward and his partners-in-crime had deleterious effects upon Langton Matravers's Parish Church of St George, which had only been rebuilt (apart from the tower) as recently as 1829. In 1874, the Reverend Trotman observed that its roof was in a, 'deplorable condition' and that, 'The wide-spanning roof... is... pushing the walls out of the perpendicular.' This, considering the extra load the barrels must have placed upon it, is not altogether surprising! The result was that the church had to be demolished and rebuilt a second time (again, apart from the tower). It was reopened in 1876.

Before judging Hayward too harshly, it is important to understand people's attitudes to smuggling in those times. The upper echelons of society were, as often as not, 'in on it': the gentlemen relying on the smugglers to supply their brandy, Geneva (gin), Madeira and Canary wines, and tobacco, and the ladies, their silk stockings and perfumes, and both for their teas, coffees, peppers and spices.

As for the labouring classes, their wages were at subsistence levels, particularly in Dorset. Also, they tended to have large families, where it was quite usual for the man, as breadwinner, to have ten or fifteen children to support (though the older ones would, of course, seek work as soon as

An elevation of St George's Church, Langton Matravers,
as it was in Hayward's time.

they were able.) Smuggling, to them, was therefore seen not as a crime, and they were anxious to avail themselves of any opportunity that came along to increase their meagre incomes.

There was also the element of excitement, which must have appealed particularly to the younger men – creeping out on a dark night to a pre-arranged landing place to signal to a French ship out in the bay; hearing the rhythmical splash of oars as the rowing boat came in with its cargo of contraband; experiencing a thrill of anticipation as dozens and sometimes hundreds of men, armed (in case of ambush by the riding officers) with clubs, knives, and even blunderbusses, hurried to unload the precious casks of spirits, 'Ells' (measures) of pepper, 'Anchors' of vinegar and 'Hogheads' of Bonea (China) tea, hiding it away in some cave or quarry prior to the journey inland. The English writer and poet Rudyard Kipling, gave a vivid portrayal of the scene in his poem 'A Smugglers Song':

If you wake at midnight,
   and hear a horse's feet.
Don't go drawing back the blinds,
   or looking in the street,
Them that asks no questions
   Isn't told a lie.
Watch the wall, my darling,
   while the Gentlemen go by!

Five and twenty ponies
   Trotting through the dark –
Brandy for the Parson,
   Baccy for the Clerk,
Laces for a lady, letters for a spy,
   Watch the wall, my darling,
while the Gentlemen go by!

Charles Hayward's secret died with him, and the truth about his smuggling activities only came to light through his grandson's diary. His double life appears not to have affected him adversely – he died on 11 May 1879, at the ripe old age of 82. There is a memorial to him in St George's Parish Church. Sadly, however, he could not be buried with his wife Rose, who predeceased him. This was because the church was rebuilt in 1875 over her grave. Hayward is, therefore, buried in the new churchyard, which opened in 1872.

7

John Mowlem: From Quarry Boy
to Stone Magnate

John Mowlem was born on 12 October 1788, at Carrant's Court (Court Hill), Swanage. His father, also John, was a quarryman, and his mother Hannah, was brought up at Ulwell Mill, Ulwell, situated on the north side of Swanage. From such humble beginnings, he would go on to found a great company.

In Mowlem's early years, his family experienced great hardship:

> I was one of six children, we were two girls and four boys, [and] a father with no one that could give or lend a penny...

(Despite this, however, his father, John senior, prospered and, according to Swanage builder and historian William Masters Hardy, came to manage, 'a general goods shop' in the town.)

The growth of the Purbeck limestone industry coincided with the decline of the Purbeck marble trade, for which the area was famous. However, whereas the marble had been hauled laboriously overland to Ower Quay on the southern shore of Poole Harbour, and thence to Poole, as far as stone was concerned, it was found far easier to transport it by ship from Swanage Bay.

Purbeck limestone was laid down in sedimentary deposits in the

John Mowlem. Photo: David Haysom Collection

Below: *Court Hill, Swanage, circa 1895, where John Mowlem was born.*
Photo: David Haysom Collection

Jurassic/Cretacious era (199-65 million years ago,) each layer being unique in its fossiliferous content. Colours range from grey/blue to cream/beige. It occurs in more than 70 varieties. The quarrymen of days gone by had a particular name for each one – 'Thornback', 'Cap and Feather', 'Roach', etc, and knew, by experience, for what purpose each variety was best suited.

The life of a quarryman was both arduous and dangerous. The men and boys who worked the multitude of small, family-owned, underground quarries, dug at an angle of 45 degrees and a depth of fifty feet or so into the Swanage hillside; hewed out the stone by the light of a candle stuck to the brim of their caps or to the wall. It was then hauled to the surface on small wooden carts, pulled by a chain attached to a capstan, which was turned by a pony or donkey harnessed to the end of a long, wooden lever – or 'spack'. The animal would walk round and round in a circle and an experienced one would keep its eye open and stop automatically when the quarry cart reached the top.

The pony resting from his labours (showing capstan with long wooden spack and chain used to haul stone up from underground). Photo: David Haysom Collection

*A stone-cart, passing the Ship Hotel, Swanage, on its way to the depots –
'bankers' – on the seafront, circa 1885.* Photo: David Haysom Collection

The stone was collected by horse-drawn stone wagons – known as 'carts' –
which made a tremendous din as they thundered through the narrow streets
of Swanage towards the seafront in a cloud of dust.

John Mowlem told WM Hardy that he himself, his father, and his three
brothers, were the last gang of quarrymen to work at Tilly Whim, situated
on the coast a mile to the south of Swanage. Working a cliff-side quarry,
such as Tilly Whim, was a different proposition from underground
quarrying inland; for here the stone was already exposed. However, in order
that it could be worked, it was necessary to create a horizontal ledge on the
cliff face, from where it was possible to burrow into it, great pillars being
left to support the roof. Blocks of stone obtained in this way were then
lowered from the ledge using a derrick – known as a 'whim' – into boats
('lighters') waiting below. It was then rowed around the coast to Swanage.

Here, the stone was taken to the seafront and stored in the open air in repositories known as 'bankers', at each of which, fifty or so men were employed. Their task was to cut the stone into appropriate shapes for flagstones, kerbstones, building blocks, corbels, pillars, and so forth; the final smoothing and finishing – or 'dressing' – being performed using chisels and the traditional round-headed, wooden mallets. So important a commodity was stone, that there was a time when the people of Swanage chose to use blocks of it to pay for their goods, rather than use the coinage of the realm.

The Swanage stone-quarrymen and handlers were a hardy and independent breed of men. They resented outside interference, particularly from the inspectors that came down from London, who were horrified at the primitive way in which stone was moved from the 'bankers' to the ships lying in the bay. This involved the stone first being manhandled into specially constructed high-sided, horse-drawn carts, designed to enter the water from where the stone was again manhandled into waiting lighters. This involved men standing chest deep in the water, and it was not unknown in winter time, for a man to die of cold, when performing this operation. It is not unusual even today, after a storm, for clay pipes to be washed up on Swanage beach, and one can imagine that these might have belonged to the poor, shivering stone-loaders, who were obliged to smoke to keep themselves warm. Finally, the lighters ferried the stone into deeper water, to be loaded into larger sailing ships which conveyed it along the coast to destinations such as Portsmouth and Ramsgate, or up the River Thames to London.

In 1806, when he was 17 years old, John Mowlem left Swanage to seek his fortune elsewhere. The idea for this may have come from Henry Manwell. Quarryman George Manwell and his wife Ann were acquaintances of the Mowlems, and had two daughters, Susannah and Laetitia, and a son Henry, who worked, first in Hampshire, and later in London, as a stone cutter engaged on government business. Alternatively, Mowlem may have been

Stone being transferred from a cart into a lighter, before being transferred to the larger vessel waiting further out to sea. Photo: David Haysom Collection

encouraged in his ambitions by Swanage's Scottish educationalist and rector the Reverend Andrew Bell.

According to Mowlem's nephew George Burt, about whom more will be said later, Mowlem first found employment at Norris Castle on the Isle of Wight, where architect James Wyatt – English architect specialising in the neoclassical style – recommended him to Henry Westmacott, sculptor/ mason of Pimlico, London. How did someone as lowly as Mowlem come to the attention of Wyatt, an architect of renown? Perhaps the influential Dr Andrew Bell, Rector of Swanage, had something to do with it!

Under Westmacott, Mowlem achieved rapid promotion to foreman of all the works in the capital in which his firm was involved. However, finding Westmacott a parsimonious employer whose wages were not 'enough to live on,' Mowlem left his employ, having worked for him for seven years. In

1812, Mowlem married Susannah Manwell at the Parish Church of St George, Hanover Square, Mayfair, London.

By 1823, Mowlem had created a firm of his own, 'John Mowlem and Company'. In the words of WM Hardy:

> At that time, the streets, roads, and alleys of London were in a very bad condition, mostly pitched with pebbles, great round stones obtained from the beach at different parts of the coast. So dirty were they that the Londoners made up their minds to have new and better roads. And Mr Mowlem bore an important part in this work.

Not only that, but, 'year after year brought him increase of prosperity.'

Mowlem leased a wharf in Pimlico Basin, off the Grosvenor Canal which ran from the River Thames to Pimlico (a 'basin' being an open area of water enclosed by dock gates and lined with wharves and warehouses, where

An early type of scarifier, used for road maintenance in London in the 1860s. It bears the name 'Mowlem, Burt and Freeman.' Photo: Poole Museum Service

barges and other vessels could unload goods and supplies). He now began importing limestone from Purbeck, sandstone from York, and granite from Aberdeen – the raw materials which he needed in order to ply his trade. In that year, 1823, as befitted his growing status, he had his portrait painted by Ramsay Richard Reinagle, RA. He subsequently established his headquarters at Paddington Basin, terminus of the Grand Junction Canal which ran from Northamptonshire to the River Thames.

Mowlem's first major contract was to repave the roadway across the River Thames's Blackfriars Bridge (completed 1769,) which required granite paving blocks – or 'setts' – the granite being obtained from quarries which he owned in the Channel Island of Guernsey.

In 1845, at the age of 57, Mowlem retired and returned with his wife to Swanage. When he did so, he observed, regretfully, that over the past sixty years, 'not a single improvement' had occurred to the town. Yet he was thankful that, 'God Almighty has spared my life to improve the place where I first drew breath.' The couple purchased a property: Number 2, Victoria Terrace, which was recently built and near to the seafront. In its roof, he built an 'observatory', from which fine views of the bay could be gained. He was particularly interested in the movements of shipping, and also in astronomy and the weather. For the remainder of his life, Mowlem devoted himself to public works and to public service. He was made a Justice of the Peace, but his main preoccupation was to use his wealth and expertise to improve the infrastructure of the town.

As WM Hardy remarked:

At this time, all the roads and bridges were in a very bad state, a state hardly conceivable nowadays[s] by those accustomed to our [the] nicely-contoured surface of macadam, almost as smooth as a billiard board.

In particular, Hardy described how the stone-carrying wagons – sometimes as many as fifty a day – created ruts in the roads, which were, 'nine and ten inches deep.'

Having been appointed 'waywarden' (a person elected to supervise the highways of a parish or district) by the Vestry (committee of parishioners), Mowlem devoted himself to paving and kerbing, 'the paths of nearly all the roads, streets and lanes.' In many instances, this also involved smoothing out humps and bumps, creating drains, and building bridges. The millpond, fed by a spring, the source of the town's water, was constantly being churned up by cattle and horses which waded into it to drink. To prevent this from happening, Mowlem increased the height of the wall surrounding it, and created a flight of steps for the benefit of those who visited it to collect their water.

In 1849, the Mowlems moved to Herston House, Swanage, where, on 11 November of that year, Susannah died. She was buried at nearby Kingston, beneath a massive pyramid made of granite blocks which arrived from Guernsey in 85 packing cases. In 1854, Susannah's grave and monument were relocated to Swanage's new, Northbrook Cemetery.

In June 1851, Mowlem wrote to Mr Jardine, Magistrate of Bow Street Magistrates Court, London, requesting that he provide Swanage with a policeman. On 21 July, Officer John Cripps, described by Mowlem as, 'a fine fellow', duly arrived to assume his duties.

It was chiefly by the exertions of Mowlem that, in 1859, Swanage's first wooden pier and tramway were built. This was intended to obviate the dangerous practice of men and horse-drawn wagons having to enter the water. However, in order to avoid paying the pier toll, the men preferred, in the main, to continue in their traditional way. A tramway linked the new pier with the bankers and a coal depot on the seafront. One third of a mile in length, its original gauge was the standard 4 feet 8½ inches.

Plans were made to link this tramway to the stone quarries at Langton Matravers, but due to opposition from local landowners, this did not come to pass.

Mowlem erected two monuments. The first was to Albert – known as 'The Good' – the late Prince Consort, who had died in 1861. The second was to King Alfred, and its inscription read as follows:

> In commemoration of a great naval battle fought with the Danes in Swanage Bay by Alfred the Great, AD.877.

In fact, historians now believe it to be more likely that the Danish fleet was wrecked by a storm. Mowlem placed on the top of his monument a cluster of four bomb shells which had been found lodged in the wooden hulls of British ships returned from the Crimean War. This gives the false impression that Alfred used cannon balls to defeat the Danes, even though the event took place five centuries before the general use of gunpowder in warfare!

In 1863, Mowlem provided the town with its 'Mowlem Institute', designed by Weymouth architect GR Crickmay, and built of stone with a roof of Welsh slate. Consisting of a museum, reading room and library, it was to be, 'for the benefit and mutual improvement of the working classes.'

As chairman of Swanage's 'Pier and Tramway Company', the indefatigable Mowlem pressed hard for Swanage to be linked by rail to the main line at Wareham, but alas, he did not live to see his dream come true. In 1868, he established the first gas works in Swanage. He died on 8 March in his eightieth year, and was buried in Northbrook Cemetery, alongside his wife.

Sequel

Today, Purbeck limestone is used, not only for building and paving work, but also decoratively, as landscaping. In its polished form, it is also used for

The 'Mowlem Institute', with stone 'bankers' in the foreground, circa 1875.
Photo: David Haysom Collection

cladding, hearths, mantles, and vanity worktops.

John Mowlem would have been much gratified to know that the company which he founded, went from strength to strength, and became 'Mowlem plc'. (In February 2006, it was taken over by 'Carillion plc' of Wolverhampton.)

8

George Burt: Further Transforming the Face of Swanage

George Burt, born in 1816, was John Mowlem's nephew; his father Robert, a Swanage stonemason, having married Laetitia, sister of Mowlem's wife Susannah. The Burts were stone and coal merchants, and they also owned a bakery. Like Mowlem, Burt had served his apprenticeship in the Swanage quarries.

Mowlem appreciated Burt's, 'good business qualities, shrewdness, fine character and energy of nature.' In 1835, he invited the 19-year-old to come to London and join him and his colleague Joseph Freeman, a Yorkshire stonemason at the firm.

In 1839, Freeman married Burt's eldest sister Elizabeth. In 1841, Burt himself married Elizabeth Hudson. The couple had six children. In 1844, Mowlem took Burt and Freeman into partnership, and created the firm 'Mowlem, Freeman and Burt'. In 1850, Burt purchased a house in Paddington; in 1857, he purchased Purbeck House – a Georgian building situated in the High Street, Swanage – for £550.

The work of the firm in improving and widening the streets of London, involved the removal of many unwanted bollards and lamp standards. Instead of leaving such objects to gather dust in the firm's stone-yard, the imaginative Burt saw that they could fulfill a dual function. They could be used as ballast for the empty ship returning from London to Swanage to

George Burt. Photo: David Haysom Collection

Purbeck House, Swanage, circa 1910.
Photo: David Haysom Collection

collect more stone, and they could also come in useful in Swanage itself, by bringing to the town a flavour of the capital. As a result, some would refer to Swanage as 'Little London by the sea.'

The bollards, which Burt transferred from London and re-erected in Swanage, were in fact replica cannons. Made of cast iron, each was embossed with the name of the London street and parish from which it came. As for the cast-iron lamp standards, they could also be put to good use, now that Swanage had a gas supply.

81

To publicise his stone merchant's business, and to impress his wealthy clients, the flamboyant Burt, in 1862, purchased the land between the town's High Street and the coast, and here he created the Durlston Park Estate. It would be self-contained with houses, church, shops and a castle.

Adorning the massive walls of the castle, which was also designed by GR Crickmay, are stone tablets inscribed with information about astronomy, and also about tidal movements at various locations around the coast. Elsewhere, there are cliff-side walks, punctuated with stone seats and more inscribed tablets, this time of a poetical nature.

In 1864, Burt was successful in having an Act of Parliament passed which would enable pure water to be supplied to his new Durlston Park Estate. To this end, a water tower, which came into operation in 1886, was built on the hill on the south side of the town.

Thomas Docwra was a retired London contractor and a friend of George Burt. His home was 'The Grove' – a six-bedroomed mansion overlooking Swanage Bay. When Burt presented Dowcra with the Wellington Clock Tower, the latter decided to erect it in the grounds of his house, and it was Mowlem's firm who shipped it from London to Swanage. The tower, designed by architect Arthur Ashpital, had been built in 1854 as a memorial to Irish-born soldier and statesman Arthur Wellesley, 1st Duke of Wellington. Mowlems however, had removed it from its location at the southern approach to London Bridge, where it was causing an obstruction to traffic. Sadly, its 4-dialled clock, which had been displayed at the Great Exhibition of 1851, did not accompany it to Swanage. In 1874, Mowlems won its largest contract to date – to rebuild London's Billingsgate Fish Market.

In 1875, with the advice of architect Crickmay, Burt rebuilt Purbeck House to a design which was on the grand scale, with no expense spared. Incorporated into the building were tiles from the old Houses of Parliament (destroyed by fire in 1834,) and iron columns and stone balustrading with decorative iron panels from Billingsgate Fish Market. The building was faced with granite chippings – waste material left over when Mowlems constructed the steps of the Albert Memorial. Commissioned by Queen Victoria in memory of her late husband Prince Albert of Saxe-Coburg-Gotha, who had died in 1861, the memorial was erected in Kensington Gardens. It was completed in 1882.

For the floor of Purbeck House's entrance hall, Burt had a copy made of a Roman pavement, which Mowlems had unearthed in London during road-building excavations. Finally, the newly-built Purbeck House was topped off with a golden weathervane in the shape of a fish, another relic from Billingsgate Market.

The garden of Purbeck House was equally grandiose: the temple boasting eight Doric columns, which originated from the former toll-houses at Waterloo Bridge. There were also statues, busts, gargoyles (some from the Royal Exchange – where trade was regulated and controlled, credit guaranteed, and loans raised), a scale model of Cleopatra's Needle, and the jawbone of a whale! Even the stables were ornate, boasting a frieze of prancing horses, the design of which was copied from the Parthenon Temple, Athens.

Burt's magnum opus was his Great Globe. Made of Portland stone and weighing 40 tons, it was constructed in fifteen sections in the company's stone-yard at Greenwich in 1887. It was then shipped to Swanage and re-erected on a site below the castle. As a backdrop, Burt erected yet more stone tablets; this time inscribed with quotations from the Holy Bible, and from Shakespeare and other poets. Several cannons were also positioned close by.

In 1881, Burt demolished some old cottages in Swanage High Street in order to build a Town Hall on the site. Once again, the architect would be GR Crickmay. By a stroke of good fortune, the Mercer's Company of

The 'Great Globe', circa 1890. Photo: David Haysom Collection

Swanage station and staff, 1887. Photo: David Haysom Collection

London had recently made some alterations to their hall in Cheapside, and had decided to dispense with its old façade (which had been designed by Edward Jerman, in 1668.) Two storeys in height, and made of Portland stone, it exhibited, in the words of author O Newbold, 'a strange mêlée of classical features that exhale the strong Dutch flavour which dominated our architecture in the years before it came under the refining hand of Wren.' Just the very item, thought Burt, for the façade of my new town hall at Swanage!

In his time, Mowlem had campaigned vigorously for Swanage to be linked to the London & South Western Railway (LSWR) by branch line to Wareham. His dream was only fulfilled after his death, when it was left to Burt and others to promote the Swanage Railway. This required an Act of Parliament, which was passed in 1881. Finally, in 1885, the first passenger-carrying steam locomotive arrived at Swanage's spanking new railway station. The privately owned Swanage Railway Company would now run the line for one year, after which its running and maintenance would be taken over by the LSWR. (It was intended that the

The Town Hall, Swanage.

tramway which ran along the seafront from the 'bankers' to the pier head, should be linked to the new, Swanage branch. This did not come to pass.)

The arrival of the railway in Swanage in 1885 (together with the increasing use of brick in building construction,) marked the beginning of the decline of the Swanage stone industry.

The good people of Swanage were not slow to realise that catering for the visitors brought by the railway and also by the fleet of paddle steamers which plied between Poole, Bournemouth, Weymouth, and the Isle of Wight, was a far easier proposition than slogging away hewing stone in the quarries! Similarly, the shipping fleet, which was in any case unable to compete with road and rail transport, also declined.

The paddle steamer Balmoral *at Swanage Pier, circa 1906. This was one of many which used to ply between Weymouth, Swanage, Poole, Bournemouth and the Isle of Wight.* Photo: David Haysom Collection

Hitherto, the people of Swanage had obtained their drinking water from wells – a method which was now considered to be unhygienic. The problem was solved by Burt, who constructed a reservoir on the hillside at Ulwell. This gave him the excuse to erect yet another monument, this time in the form of a granite obelisk brought from London.

By now, Burt's reputation, and also his fortune, were made, and in 1892, when he and Dorset's author and poet Thomas Hardy, were introduced to one another at a meeting of the Dorset Natural History and Antiquarian Field Club, the great man of letters described the former (albeit tongue in cheek) as 'The King of Swanage'.

Not everyone was impressed by the efforts of Mowlem and Burt. English surgeon Sir Frederick Treves, for example, in his *Highways and Byways in Dorset*, spoke of the, 'certain unwonted features' and 'miscellaneous oddments' which had appeared in Swanage. He was particularly scornful of the, 'puffy cherubs holding garlands' which adorned [if that is the correct word] the façade of the Town Hall, and the 'finicking, dandified, and townish' Wellington Clock Tower.

There is more than one use for a stone-cart, as this bridal couple would have happily testified! (Note the name 'Burt', on the wagon.) The driver with his cap and whip would be wearing sturdy boots and the traditional 'moleskin' trousers.
Photo: David Haysom Collection

Burt died on 18 April 1894 at Purbeck House, at the age of 77. He was buried in Kensal Green Cemetery, London, alongside his wife Elizabeth who had predeceased him.

One may imagine both Mowlem and Burt, in their heyday, hopping around their London stone-yards like magpies, picking up a statue here, and a bollard or an obelisk there, and thinking to themselves, 'Ah yes, that would go very nicely down in Swanage!' Whatever one may think about the pair, and about their eccentric tastes, there is no doubt that without their influence, the Swanage of today would be a far less colourful and interesting place.

Sequel
1897 saw the official opening of a new Swanage pier which heralded the advent of an even greater number of tourists, anxious to enjoy themselves, spend their money, and take trips by paddle steamer across the bay.

The Burt family vacated Purbeck House after World War I, and in 1935 it became a convent.

Today, those stone quarries which still exist are primarily in the Acton/Langton Matravers area to the west of the town.

In January 1972, the Wareham to Swanage railway was closed by British Rail, and the track lifted. In the same year, the Swanage Railway Society was formed. Its team of volunteers proceeded to relay the track, and by 1995, the line had reached Norden, to the north of Corfe Castle. Since then, it has proved to be hugely successful tourist attraction.

Both Mowlem and Burt would have been gratified to know that their firm went from strength to strength, first as Mowlem plc and now as Carillion plc. Amongst the projects in which the firm has recently participated are London's NatWest Tower, the new London Bridge, the London City Airport, and the Docklands Light Railway.

9

William Brown,
Swanage Lifeboatman

Williams Brown, aged 44, fisherman and shopkeeper of Swanage, Dorset was tragically drowned on active service on 12 January 1895. Before his story is told, a brief history of the evolution of life-saving services in the area will be given.

The coast of Purbeck can be a dangerous one for the following reasons. Here can be found precipitous and unforgiving cliffs which give the mariner who is shipwrecked on them, little chance of survival. Ledges of rock project far out to sea, lurking just beneath the surface and ready to rip the bottom out of an unsuspecting vessel. The Peveril Ledges to the south side of Swanage Bay are a particular hazard, and over the centuries many ships have been wrecked there and lives have been lost within a short distance of land. Around rocky promontories, such as Handfast Point on the north side of Swanage Bay, the sea is apt to swirl turbulently, especially when the tide is on the full. Vessels which are caught up in such tidal 'races' may be carried off course, or even capsize.

William Brown. Photo: Janet Brown

89

The Coastguard station at Peveril Point, 1904.
Photo: David Haysom Collection

One of the worst shipwrecks in the area occurred on the night of 6 January 1786, when the 758 ton East Indiaman *Halsewell*, en route from Gravesend to Bengal, struck the rocks between Seacombe and Winspit. Over 160 people were lost, including Captain Pierce, out of a total of 250.

The Coastguard Service was officially established in 1822, its purpose being to prevent smuggling – an activity which caused a drain on the exchequer through lost revenues.

In 1829, the first 'Coastguard Instructions' were issued, and included in them was a section dealing with life saving and life-saving equipment. Subsquently, the protection of shipping also came within the coastguards' remit, as in recent times, did the safeguarding of the environment.

Shortly afterwards, Coastguard (or 'Watch and Preventive') stations were established in Purbeck, at Swanage, St Aldhelm's Head, Worbarrow and Kimmeridge. These stations were provided with rope-carrying mortars. Designed by Captain George Manby, the mortar was designed to fire a ball – to which a lifeline was attached – into the rigging of a stricken ship. Those in distress could then make the lifeline fast and use it to haul themselves to safety.

In 1824, the Royal National Institution for the Preservation of Lives from Shipwreck (RNIPLS) was founded, and the following year, the Dorset branch of the Institution was formed.

The mortar was heavy and cumbersome, and it took time to assemble. Also, because of the weight of the shot, the lifeline, if it missed its target, was difficult to retrieve. It was superceded, in 1842, by the Dennett rocket. Invented by John Dennett, it resembles the type used in firework displays: easily portable and quick to assemble, it could be conveyed swiftly to the place where it was needed.

In 1854, the RNIPLS became the Royal National Lifeboat Institution. In Purbeck, a lifeboat station was established at Chapman's Pool in 1866, and at Kimmeridge in 1868. However, in such remote places, men could not be found to crew the vessels; so within a few years the stations had to be abandoned.

When the brigantine *Wild Wave* was driven onto the Peveril Ledge on Swanage's south shore in 1875, the five crew were obliged to spend a terrifying night aboard as heavy seas broke over the vessel, before they could be rescued the following day. It was this incident which prompted Swanage to petition the Royal National Lifeboat Institution for a lifeboat.

Swanage's first lifeboat, a rowing boat called the *Charlotte Mary*, served the town from 1875 to 1890, and in that period saved no less than 18 people from the sea. (The original lifeboat house and slipway, built in 1875 at a cost of £350 and £175 respectively, have since been completely rebuilt on several occasions.) The record of those first years, taken from a plaque on the wall of the Swanage Lifeboat Station, reads as follows –

Lives Saved

1876 Sept 30th   Schooner *Maid of Kent* of London   5
Yacht *Dragon* of Swanage   2
1879 Jan 7th   Ketch *Effort* of Portsmouth   2
1883 Sept 1st   Yawl *Thalia* Remained by vessel and saved   5
1889 March 7th   Schooner *William Maskill* of Goole   4

It is also recorded that the Swanage lifeboat 'assisted to save' the *Maid of Kent*, and 'rendered assistance' to the smack *Aries* during this period.

William Brown was a member of the crew of the *Charlotte Mary* and must, therefore, have participated in some, possibly all, of the above rescues.

The launching of Swanage lifeboat William Erle *(I), 28 December 1890.*
Photo: David Haysom Collection

Meanwhile, Trinity House (General Lighthouse Authority for England, Wales, the Channel Islands and Gibraltar) acknowledged the danger posed by this section of coastline by building a lighthouse at Anvil Point on the cliff top south of Swanage. It was opened on 28 September 1881.

In 1890, the *Charlotte Mary* was replaced by a larger lifeboat, the *William Erle*, which had 12 oarsmen. However, this boat was found to be unstable; did not participate in any rescues, and was itself replaced, three years later, by a new *William Erle. William Erle* (II), a self-righting lifeboat built by Harland and Wolfe of Belfast at a cost of £584, was 37 feet long and 9 feet wide. She was a rowing-and-sailing boat, with two masts and 12 oarsmen.

Brown was on his second rescue mission as coxswain of the new Swanage lifeboat *William Erle* (II), when she was called to assist the Norwegian barque *Brilliant* of Grinstad. En route to the German port of Bremen with a cargo of cedar wood from Nuevitas in Cuba, *Brilliant* had been driven onto the Hook Sands, a notorious sandbank at the mouth of Poole Harbour. It was 2 pm on 12 January 1895, when the lifeboat was launched. A gale was blowing from the south-east, the sea was rough, and it was snowing. More difficult conditions can hardly be imagined.

As the *William Erle*, under sail, approached the Old Harry Ledge beneath the Old Harry Rocks, the sea became more turbulent. Suddenly, she was struck by a succession of breaking waves, which caused her first to broach (veer side-on to the waves) and then to capsize. When she righted herself, it was discovered that two men had been washed overboard. These were lifeboatmen William Smith, who was seized and hauled back aboard, and Coxswain Brown, who had been swept away and had disappeared from sight.

In the chaos, the crew struggled to regain control of the vessel. In this, they were hampered by the fact that the lifeboat's foremast was damaged. Unable to make headway, and in danger either of another capsize or being blown against the cliffs, Second Coxswain George Weeks, who had assumed command, made the decision to turn back. Brown's body was discovered washed up on the shore at Studland the following day.

Fortunately for the crew of the *Brilliant*, Poole's *Boy's Own No.2* lifeboat had also been summoned to the scene, to which she was towed by the steam tug *Telegraph*. The outcome was that all *Brilliant*'s crew members were rescued, including Captain Bjerke. The ship, however, was now a wreck.

There is a plaque in the present day Swanage Lifeboat House which testifies to Brown's bravery, and states that the sum of £2,162 10s 2d was raised by public subscription, 'for the benefit of the orphans and widow of William

Robert Brown in 1895, aged 3. (Boys wore dresses until the age of 3, when they were put into breeches – 'breeched'.) Photo: Janet Brown

Brown.' As for the *William Erle*, she went on to rescue a total of fourteen people from the sea, before being replaced in 1914.

Sequel

William Brown's son Robert, sailed to Ireland, bringing back with him lobsters, which he introduced to the rocky ledges around Swanage.

In 1928, Swanage received its first motorised lifeboat, the *Thomas Markby*.

Swanage's *Robert Charles Brown*, named after a lifeboatman who served the Swanage station for over 50 years, is a 'Mersey Class' lifeboat which was placed on service in 1992. An 'all weather' type, its length is 12 metres. It has a crew of 6 and a range of 14 nautical miles, and cost £650,000.

Also on hand is Swanage's 'D' class *D613* inflatable lifeboat *Jack Cleare*, which was donated by Mrs Phyl Cleare, cost £25,000, and was placed on service in August 2003. At 5 metres in length and with a single outboard motor and a crew of 2/3, it can run for 3 hours at maximum speed. Small, and highly manoeuvrable, it is ideally suited to participating in rescues close to the shore.

Since William Brown's time, Swanage's lifeboats and life-savers have saved more than 600 lives.

10

George Spencer Watson RA, Painter of Distinction

George Spencer Watson, born 8 March 1869, was the son of William Spencer Watson, a surgeon and specialist in diseases of the nose and nasal sinuses. From Merchant Taylors' School, he entered the St John's Wood School of Art which prepared students for entry to the Royal Academy Schools (RAS), to which he gained admission in 1889. In the same year, he was awarded a silver medal by the RAS.

Two years later, in 1891, Watson was awarded the RAS's silver medal for drawing, and in the same year, he exhibited at the Royal Academy (RA) even though he was still only a student. In 1892, he won the Sir Edwin Landseer Scholarship (awarded in honour of English animal painter Sir Edwin Landseer).

Watson is described as, 'the typical artist – tall, bearded, and handsome…. A man of charming manners, with a fund of whimsical humour under his shy exterior.'[1] He was a quick worker who preferred to complete his works at a single sitting. When he showed his composition 'La Belle Dame' to his tutor from the RA, the painter and sculptor Frederic, Lord Leighton, he was advised to develop his own style, rather than to imitate that of other people – in this case, John William Waterhouse and the Pre-Raphaelites. That Watson heeded this advice is confirmed by the following comment:

Like many retiring people, Watson was apt to become rather reckless

'Portrait of a Painter', self portrait, by George Spencer Watson, RA.
Photo: Mary Spencer Watson

when he let himself go, indulging in violent contrasts of light and shade, and losing control of his colour. His best works were in a somewhat severe convention, incisively drawn and modelled with continuous gradations, with blacks and greys predominating in the colour scheme.[2]

In a diary which covers the years 1893-95, Watson refers to the fact that he has told his uncle, who was a clergyman, that his faith in Christianity had been replaced by his faith in Art. However, this did not prevent him from accepting commissions for works on Christian themes. For example, murals for churches, and friezes – the 'Story of Creation' and 'Three Wise Kings' (both in 1920), and 'The Adoration'. In 1897, he was admitted to the Arts Club founded by writer Charles Dickens and others in 1863, as a meeting place for artists and writers.

In a notebook, which he commenced to write in December 1900, Watson described what he believed to be his duty as a painter. The artist, he declared, 'is a sacrifice to beauty… He sees beauty, and he tries to express his joy by showing people what it is he sees.'

On 23 May 1907, Watson commenced a painting of Mrs Roger Thompson, the daughter of a Surrey merchant. In August 1908, he painted Mrs Thompson's sister Mrs Tidsall, whose portrait was greatly admired by the third sister, Miss Hilda Gardiner. To complete the trio, Watson, in 1908, painted Hilda herself, and the following October, 1909, he and she were married. Hilda had trained in Europe as a violinist. She was also a dancer and a mime artist. She would later study psychology under Swiss psychologist Carl Gustav Jung.

Having married Hilda, Watson began a new phase of his writing career. The fact that he was a family man is attested to by his many paintings of his wife and daughter, and of their horses and dogs. In 'Hilda and Maggie', for example, Hilda is, of course, his wife, and 'Maggie' – her dog. From now on, with the backdrop of the Purbeck landscape to draw upon, paintings of

George Spencer Watson painting in his studio, circa 1906.
Photo: Mary Spencer Watson

outdoor life would also become part of his repertoire.

The Watsons' only child Mary, was born on 7 May 1913. From that year onwards, they spent their holidays at Studland in Purbeck, where the scenery, with its rolling hills, heathland, sand dunes and sea, provided Watson with inspiration for landscape painting.

When World War I broke out in 1914, Watson volunteered for the armed services, but was considered, at 45, to be too old for enlistment. He, therefore, spent the war in Kensington (where he and his family lived, and where he had his studio) as a special constable. His brother (Oliver) Cyril, did serve in the War, as an army commander. Among the medals which Cyril was awarded were the Distinguished Service Order and the Victoria Cross, which was awarded posthumously, after he was killed in action.

Watson's aim was to be elected to the Royal Academy, and to this end he painted 'The Donkey Ride', which was exhibited at the RA in 1919, and considered to be the picture of the year. Sadly, this picture cannot now be traced, but it is believed to present an image (probably of Hilda and Mary) moving across the Purbeck landscape. 'Four Loves I found: A Woman, a Child, a Horse and a Hound' was painted in 1922 and depicts Watson himself, his wife Hilda and their daughter Mary (who is seated on a horse) in the Purbeck countryside, with Studland Bay and the Old Harry Rocks in the background. Between 1910 and 1925, Watson painted no less than fifteen such 'Riding pictures'.

In 1923, the family relocated to Dunshay Manor in the heart of Purbeck (where farmer and smallpox vaccinator Benjamin Jesty had lived more than a century previously). Here, Watson converted the former dairy house into a studio. The reason for the Watsons moving was that, with the advent of a new chain-link ferry across the mouth of Poole Harbour, Studland was being visited by tourists in ever increasing numbers, and the Watsons,

George in particular, who by all accounts, was a shy and nervous individual, desired to have more seclusion.

In the same year, 1923, Watson was elected Associate of the Royal Academy (ARA). He was primarily a portrait painter of the late romantic school (early 19th century) – 'Romanticism' emphasising intuition, imagination and feeling. He refused to embrace the avant garde movement of the time, whose abstract paintings he regarded as being cold and clinical. Sometimes, however, he painted in the style of the Italian Renaissance – 'Prometh[e]us Concoled' (1900), for example. His nude studies – such as 'The Fountain' (1900) and simply 'Nude' (1917), were, 'remarkable for [their] refinement of feeling.'[3]

'Dunshay' by George Spencer Watson, RA. Photo: Mary Spencer Watson

'Hilda and Maggie' by George Spencer Watson, RA.
Photo: Mary Spencer Watson

Lord Leighton had advised Watson to stick to nature; advice which he heeded, except when he was painting portraits, which he was obliged to do in order to make a living. Now, in his outdoor works, brilliant colours and uncomplicated natural beauty would be the order of the day, as in 'Ballard Down, Studland', 'September Morning', and 'Spring in the Orchard'. He also made paintings of his home, Dunshay Manor, and its immediate surroundings featuring subjects such as a yew tree, elm trees, the goat's yard, the hayrick, and the entrance gates.

Watson continued to contribute paintings to the Royal Academy from time to time. For example, 'The Three Kings' and 'The Story of Creation' in 1920;

'The Judgment of Paris' in 1932, and 'The Birth of Venus' in 1933. However, being chiefly a portrait painter, he mainly exhibited at the Royal Society of Portrait Painters (of which he was Honorary Treasurer); also at the Paris Salon, the Carnegie Institute, Hampstead Art Gallery, the Grosvenor Gallery, the New Gallery, the Glasgow Institute of Fine Art – to name but a few.

Despite his busy schedule, Watson found time to take fishing holidays with his friend Sir William Reynolds. He also served as Master of Worshipful Company of Saddlers – one of the most ancient of the City of London's livery companies.

A speech, which he made to the students of the Bournemouth School of Art in 1931, gives a rare glimpse into the mind of the artist:

'Four Loves I found: A Woman, a Child, a Horse and a Hound',
by George Spencer Watson, RA. Photo: Mary Spencer Watson

Undoubtedly, the most valuable quality in a picture is the creation of a new vision of the object, so that the picture appears to be a new thing never seen before and yet vivid, clear, easy to understand and beautiful.... Do not try to paint like any other painter. If you try very hard to get what you consider to be the beauty of the thing before you, it is your best chance of doing original work.... [Paintings] always look best.... Touching up is fatal.

As for his portrait painting, Watson, 'had the gift of making his sitters look well bred.' Perhaps this is one reason why he was sought after by such clients as Monica Boyd, Betty MaCann, Mr and Mrs Hardy Morritt of Rokeby Hall, County Durham, Miss Eileen Hawthorne, Paul Waterhouse (architect), Sir Francis Lacey (Secretary of the Marylebone Cricket Club), Sir Frederick Fry, KCVO (Master of the Merchant Taylors' Company), Sir Ernest Sanger (Chairman of the London County Council), Sir Montagu Sharpe, KC (Chairman of the Middlesex Sessions), Esther Harris, and James Harris. Two of his most endearing paintings are of Peter (later Sir Peter) Markham Scott, son of explorer Robert Falcon Scott and future naturalist, entitled 'Boy with a Bear', and 'Boy with a Goat'.

In February 1932, Watson was elected as a full member of the Royal Academy, having submitted as his diploma work two portraits, one of Hilda and one of Mary. He died on 11 April 1934.

Sequel

Just as Mary Spencer Watson's parents were creative: her father George in the field of painting and her mother Hilda in the field of dance-mime, so she herself soon discovered that she too had an innate creative talent.

Mary was aware that her family home Dunshay Manor, was situated adjacent to a seam of Purbeck marble – a highly prized material from which the interior decorative pillars of Salisbury Cathedral in Wiltshire were made. However, her primary interest was in stone, rather than in marble.

Mary Spencer Watson holding a pebble of iron grit-stone,
which was used in mediaeval times to polish Purbeck marble.

As a girl, Mary roamed the Purbeck Hills on her pony, and in so doing, she inevitably encountered the stone quarries. At one of these, quarry owner Titus Lander provided her with a hammer and chisel and showed her how stone can be worked. From then on, there was no stopping her.

Having studied locally, at Bournemouth School of Art, Mary went to the Slade School of Art, and then, following in her father's footsteps, to the Royal Academy, where she won several prizes and medals. Subsequently, she studied at the Central School of Art under English sculptor and equine painter John Rattenbury Skeaping, RA. 'Three wonderful months' were spent in Paris, working in the studio of Russian-Jewish artist and sculptor Ossip Zadkine.

Just as her father George, enjoyed painting natural subjects, so Mary enjoyed sculpting natural ones – such as animals, plants and figures. Several of these are to be seen in Purbeck, including 'Lady of the Rocks', in the Prince Albert Gardens, Swanage, and 'Figure of a Mason', in the churchyard of the Church of St George, Langton Matravers. There was also a strong spiritual dimension to Mary's work, as is evidenced by her 'Four Symbols of the Evangelists', carved from blocks of Purbeck freestone which border the processional way into the north entrance to Wells Cathedral in Somerset.

Mary died on 7 March 2006, at the age of 92.

Notes
1. *The Times*, George Spencer Watson, RA. Obituary.
2. Ibid.
3. Ibid.

Bibliography

Andrews, Kenneth R. 1964. *Elizabethan Privateering*.
    Cambridge University Press.

Blue Pool, The. 1983. Derby: English Life Publications.

Clay Boats and Clay Trade, The. 1987.
    Poole Maritime Trust Research Group.

Compton, Michael. 1981. *George Spencer Watson, 1869-1934*.
Southampton Art Gallery: Department of Leisure Services.

Guardian Unlimited. 18 March 2006.
    Obituary, Mary Spencer Watson by Brian Morley.

Hardy, William Masters. 1910. *Old Swanage*.
    Dorchester: Dorset County Chronicle Printing Works.

Hawkes, Andrew. 1995. *Lifeboatmen Never Turn Back*.
    Poole Historical Trust.

Hercock, Christine. 1992. *A History of Burt and Vick Ltd, Poole*.
    Borough of Poole Museum Service.

Hutchins, Reverend John. 1774. *The History and Antiquities of the County
    of Dorset*. Wakefield, Yorkshire: EP Publishing Ltd, in collaboration
    with Dorset County Library.

Kidner, RW. 2000. *The Railways of Purbeck*.
    Usk, Monmouthshire: The Oakwood Press.

Lewer, David (editor). *John Mowlem's Swanage Diary*.
    1990. Wincanton, Somerset: Dorset Publishing Company.

Lloyd, Rachel. 1967. *Dorset Elizabethans*. London: John Murray.

Lewer, David, and Denis Smale. 1994. *Swanage Past*.
    Chichester, West Sussex: Phillimore & Co.

Matthews, HCG and Brian Harrison. 2004.
    Oxford Dictionary of National Biography. Oxford University Press.

Morris, Jeff. 1998. *The Story of the Swanage Lifeboats*.

Newbold, O. *The Town Hall, Swanage*.

Pead, Patrick J. *Benjamin Jesty: a New Light in the Dawn of Vaccination.*
In *The Lancet*, Volume 362, Number 9401, December 20/27 2003.

Pike Bros., Fayle & Co. Ltd. Furzebrook.
Narrow Gauge Railway Society Handbook No.1.

Pike, Warburton Mayer. Obituary, *Daily Colonist*, 30 October 1915.

Rott, LTC. 1974. *The Potters' Field – A History of the South Devon Ball Clay Industry.* Newton Abbot and London: David & Charles.

Saville, RJ. 1976. *A Langton Smuggler.*
Langton Matravers Local History and Preservation Society.

Saville, RJ. 1996. *Popular Education in Langton Matravers.*
Langton Matravers Local History and Preservation Society.

Saville, RJ. 1995. *Langton Matravers.*
Langton Matravers Local History and Preservation Society.

Seale, Thomas. 2001. *Swanage Town Trail.*
Swanage: Tithe Barn Museum.

Southey, R, and CC Southey. 1844. *The Life of the Reverend Andrew Bell.*
London: John Murray.

Times, The. 12 April 1934. Obituary: *Mr Spencer Watson, RA. A Successful Portrait Painter.*

Times, The. 13 April 1934. Obituary: *Mr Spencer Watson, RA.,* by Sir William Reynolds-Stephens.

Transcript of the Examination of William Munday of Studland by Doctor Lewes on 6 February 1581 and on 17 October 1583. Public Record Office: High Court of Admiralty Documents.

Wallace, E Marjorie. 1981. *The First Vaccinator.*
Wareham and Swanage: Anglebury-Bartlett Ltd.

Wedgwood Manuscripts, catalogue of entries concerning the Pike brothers and the Purbeck clay mines. Keele, Staffordshire: Keele University Information Services.

Index

111